Advance praise for the first English edition of
Israel in Palestine: Jewish Rejection of Zionism

"Professor Rabkin exemplifies the formidable Jewish intellectual tradition of pursuing the truth, and speaking it even when to do so is to risk ostracism."

> Ambassador Chas W. Freeman, Jr.
> Former U.S. Assistant Secretary of Defense

"Yakov Rabkin meticulously dissects the contradiction at Israel's core: A state claiming to be Jewish acting opposite to Jewish ethics."

> Robert Wintemute
> Professor of Human Rights Law,
> King's College, London

"A sharp, brilliant essay."

> Michel Brouyaux
> Association Belgo-Palestinienne,
> Wallonie-Bruxelles

Copyright ©2025 by Yakov M. Rabkin

10 9 8 7 6 5 4 3 2 1

The author asserts the moral right
to be defined as the author of this work.

ISBN 979-8-9916552-9-3 (First English Paperback Edition)

Aspect Editions
Published by Diversified Graphic LLC
Atlanta, Georgia

All rights reserved. No part of this publication may be reproduced, stored in a retrieval system or transmitted, in any form or by any means, electronic, mechanical, photocopying, recording or otherwise, without the prior permission of the publisher.

Cover photograph is dedicated to the public domain:
https://commons.wikimedia.org/wiki/File:1913_Ottoman_Geography_Textbook_Showing_the_Sanjak_of_Jerusalem_and_Palestine.jpeg

Author photograph by N. Sherman

ISRAEL IN PALESTINE
Jewish Rejection of Zionism

ISRAEL IN PALESTINE

Jewish Rejection of Zionism

YAKOV M. RABKIN

Aspect Editions

MMXXV

Contents

Preface iii
   by Ambassador Chas W. Freeman, Jr.

Acknowledgements v

Palestine Before Zionist Colonisation 1

Zionism and the Palestinians 11

A New Hebrew Man 29

European Legacy and Endurance 39

Before October 7 45

Revenge and Survival 55

Impunity and Protest 65

David, Goliath and Samson 79

Strategic Conflation: Israel's Win-Win 85

Postscript 97

Further Reading 109

Preface

FEW BOOKS are both morally inspiring and intellectually stimulating. This book is both. Professor Yakov M. Rabkin, a noted historian at the University of Montreal, has courageously made his arguments cogent and persuasive. He explains in well-documented detail how Zionism arose, how it usurped the religious idea of a Jewish return to Palestine, and how it created a nationalist parody and cruel negation of Jewish values in the state of Israel.

Judaism is known for its devotion to scholarly examination of ethical issues and the pursuit of justice. Zionism is not its offspring. The idea of gathering the world's Jews in their mythical homeland was advanced by evangelical Christians centuries before it was taken up by secular Jews. Both religious Jews and the most distinguished Jewish men of science long opposed the idea of a Jewish state, especially one in the Holy Land, migration to which, according to Jewish tradition, should await the arrival of the Messiah.

Zionism's founders were godless men animated by meanspirited Eastern European nationalism, powered by antisemitic oppression in Russia, and aided and abetted by British colonialism. Theirs was a nationalism of conquest. Its amorality lives on in the Israeli militarism that has balkanized the Levant, birthed an ideology of Jewish supremacism, and culminated in shameless repudiation of both the spirit and the laws of Judaism as well as international norms and law.

Zionism aspires to transform multiple transnational

religious communities into a nationality. Zionists insist that Israel can speak for all the world's Jews and denounce criticism of Israel's increasingly depraved behavior as anti-semitism. By demanding the loyalty of Jews abroad to Israel, Zionists call into question the patriotism of Jews to their native countries. Instead of combating anti-semitism, Zionists foment it. Israel is "not good for the Jews." Its actions menace them.

I have always admired the formidable Jewish intellectual tradition of pursuing the truth and speaking it even when to do so is to risk ostracism. Professor Rabkin exemplifies this tradition and does so with uncommon erudition. This is a book from which the readers will learn much to their benefit.

> Ambassador Chas W. Freeman, Jr.,
> Former U.S. Assistant Secretary of Defense
> Exeter, New Hampshire
> May, 2025

Acknowledgements

MY DAUGHTER MIRIAM devoted much time and effort making valuable improvements and additions to the manuscript. I am deeply indebted to her for this big-hearted contribution. I also express my sincere appreciation for the comments and corrections provided by Ruth Foltz and Heather Mackenzie, who generously offered their assistance. Needless to say, I am solely responsible for any remaining errors and imperfections.

>Yakov M. Rabkin
>Montreal, Quebec
>September, 2025

I am not amongst those who claim that progress can be taken for granted, that humanity cannot go backwards.

Louis-Auguste Blanqui (1805-1881)[1]

---

1. 'Je ne suis pas de ceux qui prétendent que le progrès va de soi, que l'humanité ne peut pas reculer,' cited in Daniel Bensaïd and Michael Löwy, 'Auguste Blanqui, heretical communist', *Radical Philosophy*, 185 (May-June 2014), p. 28.

Palestine Before Zionist Colonisation

OTTOMAN PALESTINE in the mid-19th century was a largely peaceful province, a mosaic of diverse religious, ethnic and linguistic groups. The Jews living in Palestine at the time consisted of several religious communities, primarily divided into Ashkenazim and Sephardim. Ashkenazim, originally from Central and Eastern Europe, subsisted in poverty, and were mostly supported by charitable funds from Jewish communities in Europe and North America. Sephardim, on the other hand, largely descended from Spain, Portugal and North Africa. They depended less on charity and were well integrated into the local economy. While remaining devout, Sephardim showed a greater openness to the modern influences that were infiltrating Western Asia, primarily through the establishment of foreign schools, hospitals and other institutions. Ashkenazim spoke Yiddish among themselves and Arabic with others, while Sephardim used Ladino and Arabic. Arabic served as a common language for most of the region's ethnic and confessional communities, which enjoyed a certain degree of autonomy in Ottoman Palestine.

Although they lived in the Holy Land, Jews understood themselves to be in exile—a central concept in Judaism. In the Pentateuch, exile from the Promised Land is described as divine punishment for religious disobedience and transgressions of the Hebrews (they came to be called

Jews centuries later). In reality, historians deem mass expulsion unlikely; typically, it was mostly the Jewish political elite that was exiled. It is assumed that the imperial authorities, whether Babylonian or Roman, had no interest in emptying the land and losing the income that the peasants generated for the imperial treasury.

In 1922, none other than David Ben-Gurion (1886-1973), the future founder of the state of Israel, affirmed that Palestinian *fellahin* (farmers, peasants) were most likely the closest biological descendants of the Jews of the 1st century.[1] Yet, less than thirty years later, he—and all future leaders of Israel—categorically refused to comply with the United Nations' resolution to allow these Palestinians, made refugees in 1947-1949, to return to their ancestral lands and homes. For Ben-Gurion, as for the Zionist movement more broadly, Jewish settlers of European origin had replaced the indigenous population as the legitimate heirs of the biblical Hebrews.

In rabbinic Judaism, exile and redemption are spiritual concepts of universal significance. Exile refers to an imperfect state of the world, or a loss of contact with the divine presence, rather than mere physical displacement. The founding fathers of Zionism, most of whom had abandoned Judaism, reduced the concept of exile to a literal, geographical sense. This allowed them to frame their movement in terms similar to European ethnic nationalism: a call for repatriation to "their" land. However, most Jews, Muslims and Christians living in 19th century Palestine, were hardly familiar with this modern concept of nationalism.

The relationship between Jews and the Land of Israel may seem paradoxical. Although it occupies a privileged place in Jewish identity, Jews made no effort to settle there en masse before the rise of Zionism. Political scientist and historian Shlomo Avineri (1933-2023), former Director General of Israel's Ministry of Foreign Affairs, points out that:

> [...] for all of its emotional, cultural and religious intensity, the link with Palestine did not change the praxis of Jewish life in the Diaspora: Jews may pray three times a day for the deliverance that would transform the world and transport them to Jerusalem, but they did not emigrate there.[2]

For most observant Jews today, the physical concentration of millions of Jews in Israel has little to do with the messianic hope.

Moreover, it is largely understood that the divine promise to Abraham in no way implies the right to possess the Promised Land. Abraham, well aware of God's promise of the Land of Canaan, nevertheless insists on paying for a plot of land to bury his wife Sarah (Genesis 23:3-16). The Promised Land belongs not to the one who receives the promise, but rather to the one who gives it.

The origin story of the Jews differs from other founding stories. The Jews were not born as a people in "their" land. Abraham arrived in the Land of Canaan only after leaving his homeland in response to a divine command: "The Lord had said to Abraham: 'Get away from your country, your birthplace and your father's house, and go to the land I will show you.'" (Genesis 12:1). His sons and descendants, far from settling there permanently, migrated to Egypt. In other words, the biblical narrative clearly emphasises that the Jews were not "natives" of the Land of Canaan.

Judaic sources trace the origins of the Jews to the

shared experience of leaving Egypt and receiving the Torah at Mount Sinai. This group is historically defined as bound by the precepts of the Torah. Although the latter is replete with episodes of transgression and forgetfulness of Divine Law on the part of the Children of Israel, the obligation to obey the Torah remains valid. It is this relationship—and the obligation to follow the Torah's commandments—that traditionally characterise Jews as "the chosen people." This concept does not imply any intrinsic superiority, but rather denotes specific moral and ritual responsibilities. As a former Chief Rabbi of Britain once explained:

> Every people is "chosen" or destined for some distinct purpose in advancing the designs of Providence. Only, some fulfill their mission and others do not. Maybe the Greeks were chosen for their unique contributions to art and philosophy, the Romans for their pioneering services in law and government... The Jews were chosen by God to be "peculiar unto Me" as the pioneers of religion and morality; that was and is their national purpose.[3]

In the Biblical narrative, failure to fulfill such responsibilities carries consequences. As the prophet Amos declared: "You alone have I singled out of all the families of the earth—that is why I will call you to account for your iniquities." (Amos 3:2)

Of course, this concept is easily misused to justify ethnocentrism, a sense of superiority, pride and racism. Yet Jewish tradition offers a powerful antidote to such distortions, particularly through its teachings on the origins of a figure as central as the Messiah. The sages concur that the Messiah will arise from the lineage of King David, which would appear to confer upon him a superior ascendancy. However, the same sages trace King David's origin to three quite daring female initiatives—those of Lot's daughters, Ruth and Tamar (see Genesis 19:30-38, Ruth 3:7-8 and Genesis 38:1-30). Jewish tradition emphasizes the gentile origins of the Messiah, the savior of the world meant to return the Jews to the Promised Land, thereby tempering any temptation to claim "Jewish superiority." A typical example of this outlook is found in the writings of the Provençal scholar Menahem Meiri (1249-1315), a renowned rabbinic authority and philosopher, who categorically rejects any discrimination against gentiles.[4]

Most Judaic sources do not regard the gentile as ontologically different. The Talmud praises the concept of humanity's common origin—from Adam—because it helps mitigate hostility in the world. There would be many more wars if people could claim that they and their opponents were of different ultimate origins.[5]

Biblical texts emphasise not only the divine origin of the Torah, but also the fact that it was given outside the Land of Israel. According to the Hebrew Bible, the Jews—or more precisely the Children of Israel—are consecrated as a distinct people through their acceptance of the Torah at Mount Sinai. Moreover, their spiritual purification, necessary to enter the Promised Land, takes place outside of it, during the forty years of wandering in the desert. As many exegetes point out, the Holy Land cannot make Jews holy; on the contrary, their transgressions can desecrate the Land, which in turn will "vomit them out" (Leviticus 18:28). The French philosopher Emmanuel Levinas (1906-1995) expressed this idea by suggesting that the Land is *permitted* rather than *promised*—a pun that resonates more strongly in the original

French: *une terre permise plutôt que promise.*⁶

Tradition defines the relationship with the Holy Land in explicitly conditional terms:

> Beware lest your heart be seduced, and you turn astray and serve gods of others and bow to them. Then the wrath of the Lord will blaze against you. He will restrain the heaven so there will be no rain and the ground will not yield its produce. And you will swiftly be banished from the goodly land which the Lord gives you. (Deuteronomy 11:16-17)

Jewish tradition therefore underscores the great risk of living in the Holy Land by comparing the Land of Israel to a royal palace, where any transgression immediately takes on enormous proportions. A parable attributed to Rabbi Yosef Hayim Sonnenfeld (1848-1932), one of the pillars of the pious Jewish community in Palestine and a convinced anti-Zionist, illustrates the logic behind the hope of Messianic salvation:

> God has exiled us on account of our sins, and exile is as a hospital for the Jewish people. It is inconceivable that we take control of our land before we are completely cured. ... What we seek of deliverance is that our cure be complete; we seek not to return in ill health to the royal palace, God forefend.⁷

According to tradition, the Land of Israel would be acquired as part of a universal messianic project, unlike the previous two acquisitions (under Joshua and during the return from Babylonia), which relied on earthly power. The Zionist claim on Palestine is based on a literal interpretation of the Bible, one that diverges drastically from the teachings of rabbinic Judaism. It is this departure from two thousand years of Jewish tradition that, in this view, helps explain the persistent and recurring violence since the foundation of the State of Israel. In this worldview, the physical reconstruction of the Holy Land by the godless can lead only to spiritual and material destruction: "Zionism is the most terrible enemy that has ever arisen to the Jewish Nation. ... Zionism kills the nation and then elevates the corpse to the throne."[8]

The Talmud records the oaths sworn to God on the eve of the dispersion of the Jews to the four corners of the earth: not to return en masse and in force to the Land of Israel, and not to rebel against the nations.[9] For generations, long before the rise of Zionism, rabbis insisted on the full application of these Talmudic vows to reinforce the prohibition against settling in Palestine and to obligate the Jews to accept the yoke of exile. For example, the revered Maharal of Prague, Rabbi Yehuda Loew ben Bezalel (1512-1609), insisted that even under threat of massacre and torture, the Jews have no right to establish themselves in Israel, and have even less right to use force against the nations to do so.[10]

To better understand the changes brought about by Zionist colonisation of Palestine, it is important to look at how Jews have historically related to Muslims, now the majority in Palestine, over the centuries. According to one of America's most prolific experts on Judaism, Rabbi Jacob Neusner (1932-2016), "No two religions among all the religions of the world, concurring on so much, have better prospects of understanding and conciliation than Islam and Judaism."[11]

While the Hebrew Bible portrays gentiles as idolaters; the advent of Christianity and Islam led to a new kind of relationship with other religions. Jewish tradition came to see Christianity and Islam as variations of the true faith. Major Jewish thinkers appreciated both religions as vehicles for spreading the concepts of monotheism and the Messiah throughout the world.

Judaic jurists viewed Islam as a strict monotheism, free from idolatrous deviations, and affirmed that Muslim hearts are directed towards Heaven. According to the great medieval rabbinical authority and philosopher Moses Maimonides (1135-1204), also known as Abu Imran Musa bin Maimun bin Ubaydallah al Qurtubi, who held a high position in Islamic Egypt and knew Islam well, Muslims "are not idolaters, [idolatry] has long been severed from their mouths and hearts: they attribute to God a proper unity, a unity concerning which there is no doubt."[12] Consequently, according to Jewish law, Jews may enter mosques, while they are forbidden to approach idolatrous houses of prayer.

Moreover, Islamic knowledge was closely integrated with Judaic scholarly production in Muslim countries, where most Jewish scholars wrote in Arabic. Unlike Latin, Arabic was widely used in rabbinic literature because medieval Judaism borrowed many elements from Islam, among them grammar, philosophy and science. Conceptual and often terminological affinities link Judaism and Islam. Jews were also instrumental in transmitting Arabic knowledge (and its important Greek component) to Christian thinkers of the Renaissance.

Muslim judges are said to have consulted Jewish judges in certain cases. Moreover, the Qur'an has a sacred status within Judaism. For centuries, Jews in Muslim-majority countries gave their children Arabic names, such as Abdallah, Ibrahim, Ismail or Salim. This centuries-old heritage of overall good relations, with exceptions, between Muslims and Jews, stands in contrast to Israel's consistent efforts to promote Islamophobia.

Today, the majority of Palestinians are Muslim. Israel's behaviour is diametrically opposed to Judaism's normative attitude towards Muslims. The impact of the violence in Israel/Palestine on mutual perceptions between Jews and Muslims should not obscure their long experience of harmonious coexistence. Israel embodies the Eastern European ethnic nationalism fashioned at the end of the 19th century, rather than the Judaism that has developed over millennia. Relations between Jews and Muslims go back some fifteen centuries, and the traumas caused by mistreatment of Palestinians by the State of Israel are likely, provided the mistreatment ends, to be healed in the future.

NOTES

1. Shlomo Sand, *Comment le peuple juif fut inventé*. Paris: Fayard, 2008, pp. 260-262

2. Shlomo Avineri, *The Making of Modern Zionism. The Intellectual Origins of the Jewish State*. New York: Basic Books, 1981, p. 3.

3. "Jews as the Chosen People." The Spiritual Life; archive.is/6BZCU

4. Sophie Bigot-Goldblum, "The Meiri: the unversalist of Perpignan." *Mozaika*, May 7, 2020; archive.is/CtwDk

5. *Babylonian Talmud*, Treatise Sanhedrin 38a.

6. Emmanuel Levinas, *Quatre lectures talmudiqus*. Paris : Éditions du minuit, 2005.

7. Quoted in Aharon Rosenberg (ed.), *Mishkenoth haro'yim*. New York: Nechmod, 1984-1987, vol. 2, p. 441.

8. Yaakov Zur, "German Jewish Orthodoxy's Attitude toward Zionism," in: Shmuel Almog, Reinharz, Jehuda, and Shapira, Anita, eds., *Zionism and Religion*. Hanover: Brandeis University Press and University Press of New England, 1998, p. 111.

9. *Babylonian Talmud,* Treatise Ketubbot 111a.

10. Yehuda Loew ben Bezalel (Maharal), *Netzah Israël*. Jerusalem: Makhon Yerushalayim, 1997, chap. 24.

11. Jacob Neusner et al., *Judaism and Islam in Practice: A Sourcebook*. London: Routledge, 2000, p. 234.

12. *Teshuvot Ha-Rambam*, no 448.

Zionism and the Palestinians

THE FOUNDERS of Zionism rightly viewed their movement as a rupture in Jewish history. The pioneers of the colonisation of Palestine proudly proclaimed "the Zionist revolution." In the words of David Ben-Gurion:

> Zionism in its essence is a revolutionary movement. One could hardly find a revolution that goes deeper than what Zionism wants to do to the life of the Hebrew people. [*NB: he does not refer to the transformed people as "Jews" but as "Hebrews," meaning "the New Hebrew" educated in the Zionist mould.*] This is not merely a revolution of the political and economic structure—but a revolution of the very foundations of the personal lives of the members of the people. The very essence of Zionist thinking about the life of the Jewish people and on Hebrew history is basically revolutionary—it is a revolt against a tradition of many centuries helplessly longing for redemption.[1]

While the Land of Israel certainly holds a central place in Jewish tradition, it is primarily Christians, beginning in the 17th century, who sought to "ingather the Hebrews in the Holy Land." Thus, this early form of Zionism, "Zionism *avant la lettre*," was not invented by Jews but by evangelical Protestants.[2] Their aim was to hasten the Second Coming of Christ and convert Jews to Christianity. This deep affinity with evangelical Protestant beliefs helps explain the massive support the State of Israel enjoys today in the United States and other countries, where evangelical Protestants number in the hundreds of millions and are a formidable pro-Israel force.

Jewish Zionism emerged much later, toward the end of the 19th century. Among the many strands of Zionism, the dominant one is a European nationalist movement with four main aims: 1) to transform the transnational Jewish identity centred on the Torah into a national identity modeled after other European nations; 2) to develop a new vernacular, a national language, based on biblical and rabbinic Hebrew; 3) to relocate Jews from their homelands to Palestine; and 4) to establish political and economic control over Palestine. While other European nationalisms concerned themselves primarily with the struggle for political and economic sovereignty, Zionism set itself the far greater challenge of trying to achieve the first three objectives: redefining Jewish identity, language and geography. It's not surprising that, at the time, the Zionist idea seemed innovative, even daring, and it repelled the majority of Jews.[3]

The first proto-Zionist settlers arrived in Palestine in the 1880s, over a decade before the political crystallisation of Zionism. Ahad Ha-Am, the pen name of Asher Hirsch Ginzberg (1856-1927), a Russian Jew and a leading intellectual in Zionist circles, deplored the cruelty these early settlers displayed towards the indigenous population of Palestine. In an article published in St. Petersburg after a visit to Palestine in 1891, he lamented the "reprehensible behaviour" of the settlers, who provoked the anger and hatred of the native population. Ahad Ha-Am's rebuke made no difference. More than a decade later, a concerned settler, speaking at the Zionist Congress, pointed out the "flagrant error" of his comrades towards the Arabs. "When we enter our land we must forget any idea of conquest or deportation."[4]

Sigmund Freud (1856-1939) attributed the violence of the 1929 Arab revolt to the "unrealistic fanaticism of our people" and refused to sign a public address that placed the blame solely on the native Arab population. These warnings and criticisms, along with thousands of others voiced to this day, have not improved the situation on the ground. Rather, they serve as a moral counterpoint to Israel's ongoing mistreatment of the indigenous population and continue to embody the chasm between the Zionists' addiction to violence and the Jewish rejection of the idolatry of power.

Admittedly, the Hebrew Bible, including the books of Joshua and Judges, is full of violent imagery. But far from glorifying war, Jewish tradition sees loyalty to God, not military prowess, as the main reason for the victories mentioned in the Bible. Developed in the absence of political power, Jewish tradition abhors violence and reinterprets the many episodes of war in the Hebrew Bible through a pacifist lens. The tradition clearly favours compromise and accommodation, values that have not been abandoned under the influence of secularisation.

Thus, Albert Einstein (1879-1956) openly denounced Betar, the paramilitary Zionist youth movement historically affiliated with the ruling Likud party. He considered it "as dangerous for our youth as Hitlerism was for the German youth."[5] In 1946, he wrote:

> I am in favor of Palestine being developed as a Jewish Homeland but not as a separate State. It seems to me a matter for simple common sense that we cannot ask to be given the political rule over Palestine where two thirds of

the population are not Jewish. What we can and should
ask is a secured bi-national status in Palestine with free
immigration.⁶

This idea remains as valid today as when Einstein, alongside other prominent Jewish figures, advanced it. Historians, in Israel and elsewhere, have pointed out that Jews lived more peacefully in Palestine before the arrival of the Zionists. According to the testimony of a German officer attached to the Ottoman army during the First World War:

> The Zionists residing there represented no more than
> 5 percent of the population, but were very active and
> fanatical, and terrorized the non-Zionists. During the
> war, the non-Zionists attempted to free themselves from
> Zionist terror with the aid of the Turks. They rightly
> feared that the activities of the Zionists would destroy
> their good relations that prevailed among long-time
> Jewish residents in Palestine and the Arabs.⁷

In fact, many Jews feared such disruption from the very beginning of the Zionist settlement.

The collapse of multinational empires in the wake of the First World War gave free rein and political expression to nationalist sentiment, resulting in several new states being formed in Central and Eastern Europe in the aftermath of the war. In 1917, Great Britain, which not only retained its Empire but also aimed to extend it into West Asia, declared its support for the idea of a "Jewish national home in Palestine" through the Balfour Declaration. In this sense, Zionism was an integral part of the European colonial enterprise. At the time, colonialism carried no negative connotations for Europeans; for example, the main financial arm of the Zionist movement was called the Jewish Colonial Trust (known today as Bank Leumi).

Zionism is a European project rooted in the ethnic nationalisms of Eastern and Central Europe. These ideologies assert that nations must live in their "natural" environment, and those outside the titular ethnic group are, at best, tolerated. Exclusive aspects of this kind of nationalism influenced the early Zionists, a legacy that remains significant today. "Zionists both reacted against and emulated such [...] nationalisms and violence."[8] In other words, they opposed them in Europe, where Jews suffered under exclusionary nationalism, and replicated them in Palestine, where they stood to benefit from it. This commitment to eliminating the native population has earned Zionism continued respect and admiration from racists and ethnic nationalists around the world.

The fact that Israel now inspires many right-wing and far-right parties globally speaks for itself. Israeli society has consistently shifted to the right due to the exclusive ethnic nationalism that is the foundation of its political structure and culture. The current assault on Gaza logically stems from the entire history of Zionism in Palestine. While it has repelled quite a few Jews, Israel has consolidated foreign support from a whole range of right-wing extremists, racists and antisemites. These include white supremacists in the United States, Islamophobes in Europe, and Hindu nationalists in India.[9]

This militaristic culture posed a particularly acute problem for the German Jews who arrived in Palestine in the 1930s fleeing the Nazi regime. They knew how to recognise fascism and saw that Nazis treated Zionists more favourably than other Jews. Moreover, a high SS official visited Zionist colonies in Palestine in the 1930s, and a medal was coined in honour of that visit.[10] To ensure the cooperation of the Nazi authorities, Zionists in Germany proudly displayed their devotion to their own form of nationalism. In this vein Kurt Tuchler, a leader of the German Zionist Federation, invited Baron Leopold Edler von Mildenstein, a high-ranking SS officer, to write pro-Zionist articles for the Nazi press. The baron, "an ardent Zionist" who had attended Zionist congresses and would later recruit Adolf Eichmann to the *Sicherheitsdienst* (SD, the Nazi security service) Jewish Desk, agreed on condition that he first visit the Zionist colonies in Palestine. The two men, accompanied by their spouses, set out shortly after Hitler's rise to power:

> What had brought them together on this journey to Palestine was their common desire, motivated by radically different objectives, to make Germany "free of Jews," or as the Nazis put it, *Judenrein*. Where the National Socialists had not yet worked out a solution to "the Jewish question," the Zionists, with their ambition to establish a Jewish homeland and their sponsorship of Jewish emigration to Palestine, had an answer.[11]

The SS official visited agricultural colonies and prominent Zionist activists, signed the guest book at the National Jewish Library[12] and duly wrote a series of laudatory articles about the Zionist enterprise in Palestine. They were published in the newspaper *Der Angriff*, founded and supported by Joseph Goebbels. A medal was coined to commemorate the visit. It carried the inscription *"Der Nazi färht nach Palästina"* (A Nazi travels to Palestine) and had a Swastika on one side and a Star of David on the other. Von Mildenstein was promoted to head the SS Jewish desk to implement his policy "to assist the expansion of Zionist influence among Germany's Jews who, despite the oppressive conditions under which they lived, still showed no great desire to emigrate to Palestine."[13] Herzl was right when he wrote that "the antisemites will become our most loyal friends, the antisemite nations will become our allies."[14]

Conversely, many German Jewish immigrants in Palestine abhorred ethnic nationalism, militarism and espoused liberal, universalist values. They were offended by the Zionists' nationalist arrogance and the resulting dehumanisation of Arabs. Well-educated and often renowned professionals, they contributed massively to Palestine's industrial and cultural development, but they could hardly be found in Zionist or later Israeli politics.

Indeed, in contrast to Jews from Eastern and Central Europe, German and American Jews with liberal values were prominent in the ranks of Jewish-Arab coexistence movements. Many of them did not identify with the muscular, proud "New Hebrew," whose image too closely resembled the Nazi Aryan ideal. After decades living in Palestine, Judah Magnes (1877-1948), president of Hebrew University and an American Reform rabbi, bitterly remarked: "It is becoming more and more difficult to be a Jew and to remain true to the spirit of Israel [Jewish ethical tradition] among these new-fashioned Hebrews."[15] Albert Einstein similarly warned that the party that would be elected in 1977 to govern Israel,

> is closely akin in its organization, methods, political philosophy and social appeal to the Nazi and Fascist parties ... Today they speak of freedom, democracy and anti-imperialism, whereas until recently they openly

preached the doctrine of the Fascist state. It is in its actions that the terrorist party betrays its real character; from its past actions we can judge what it may be expected to do in the future.[16]

Given the cult of aggressive masculinity embedded in Zionist education, the genocide in Gaza was predictable. In addition, Zionist settlers who consistently provoked Arab Palestinians have been blamed for failing to save Jews from the Nazi genocide. In 1937, when Jews were fleeing Nazi Germany, Judah Magnes wrote: "With the permission of the Arabs we can welcome into the Arab countries hundreds of thousands of Jews."[17]

Rabbi Joseph Zvi Duschinsky (1868-1948), representing the traditional Ashkenazi community before the United Nations in 1947, declared that Zionism had been the root cause of violence and friction with the Arabs—friction which led the British government to restrict Jewish immigration to Palestine from 1930 on. Zionism, in this view, was presented as an obstacle to the salvation of millions of Jews from the Nazi genocide:

> The colossal massacre of millions of our brethren at the hands of Nazism during the Second World War might have been averted to a very substantial degree for many of them might have been able to live peacefully in the Holy Land as there would have been not the slightest justification for the limitations of Jewish immigration as have in fact been enforced during the last decade.[18]

Duschinsky had unerringly singled out Zionist militancy, holding it responsible for the White Paper adopted by the British authorities that imposed severe restrictions on Jewish immigration to Palestine on the eve of World

War II. As a result, millions of Jews in Nazi-occupied Europe were condemned to death.

The unilateral proclamation of the State of Israel in 1948 by the Zionist minority, against the will of the local population, including Muslims, Christians, and many Jews, intensified the discrimination, dispossession and deportation of hundreds of thousands of Palestinians, leading to endless cycles of violence. Prominent German-speaking Jewish figures such as philosopher Martin Buber (1878-1965), political scientist Hannah Arendt (1907-1995), educator Ernst Simon (1900-1988), and physicist Albert Einstein opposed the idea of a separate state for Jews. So did Magnes who, when threatened by Zionists for his views, resigned from the Hebrew University and returned to the United States in 1948. In his farewell address to the university, he lamented that Jews throughout the world, but especially in the United States, "are subject to a Zionist totalitarianism that seeks to subjugate everyone to its discipline, and if necessary by force and violence."[19]

Indeed, this totalitarian trend shows no signs of abating. Historian Eli Barnavi, former Israeli ambassador to Paris, warned that "the dream of a 'Third Kingdom of Israel' could only lead to totalitarianism."[20] While one may question Israel's policies, rejection of Zionism is denounced as antisemitism. Jews who dare to reject it are ostracised from mainstream Jewish communities and dismissed from community institutions, fired from universities and purged from the media and government agencies. Israel's assault on Palestinians, which intensified significantly in 2023, has made pro-Israeli circles particularly aggressive towards any dissenting Jews, who are qualified as "self-hating."

Zionist supremacy is ensured at all costs, including the suppression of democratic freedoms on the pretext of fighting antisemitism, both in Israel and in Israel-allied nations.[21] Today, Israel, including local agents in many Western countries, have successfully pressured governments to suppress opposition to Israel under the guise of fighting antisemitism.[22] Members of Betar, a group once denounced by Einstein as Hitlerite, have assaulted anti-genocide demonstrators and actively cooperated with police to hound pro-Palestinians activists in the United States and other Western countries. Additionally, a number of prominent Israeli politicians have proudly declared themselves racist and fascist (see below).

In Israel, the settler-colonial nature of the state, and the resulting systemic decades-long oppression of Palestinians, and now genocide, not only discredits democratic pretences in the country's political culture. This reality also complicates long-held assumptions, such as the belief that victims of historical injustice cannot become perpetrators. Vladimir Jabotinsky (1880-1940), a Russian writer, admirer of Mussolini and founder of the political movement that produced Benjamin Netanyahu (whose Russian-born father was Jabotinsky's secretary), wrote an essay characteristically titled "Homo homini lupus" (Man is a Wolf to Man). In 1910 he expressed a political philosophy that explains the genocide in Gaza:

> Sometimes we base too many rosy hopes on the fallacy that a certain people has itself suffered and will therefore feel the agony of another people and understand it and its conscience will not allow it to inflict on the weaker people what had been earlier inflicted on it. But in reality it appears that these are mere pretty phrases ... Only the

Bible says "you shall not oppress a stranger; for you know the heart of the stranger, seeing you were strangers in the land of Egypt." Contemporary morality has no place for such childish humanism.[23]

Unlike Netanyahu, Jabotinsky never claimed Jewish exceptionalism in moral or political conduct.

Questions about whether pacifist values are firmly anchored in the Jewish worldview or are instead shaped by historical circumstances were raised almost a thousand years ago by the Spanish poet, scholar, and rabbi Yehuda Halevi (1080-c.1141). In his philosophical work *The Kuzari*, written as a defense of Judaism, Halevi presents a dialogue between a rabbi and a king seeking a religion for his kingdom. The rabbi says:

> I see thee reproaching us [for] degradation and poverty, but the best of other religions boast of both. Do they not glorify Him who said: "He who smites thee on the right cheek, turn to him the left also; and he who takes away thy coat, let him have thy shirt also?" He and his friends and followings, after hundreds of years of flogging and slaying attained their well-known success, and just in these things they glorify. This is also the history of the founder of Islam and his friends, who eventually prevailed, and became powerful.

To which the king responds with a touch of cynicism: "This might be so, if your humility were voluntary; but it is involuntary, and if you had power, you too would slay."[24] The king suggests that if Jews held political or military dominance, as other nations, they too might act as violently. In other words, Halevi's dialogue explores the idea that pacifist values may not stem from moral conviction but from lack of power. It is striking that such reflections were articulated nearly a millennium before the founding of the State of Israel.

For many devout individuals, the abdication of political power in the Land of Israel is seen to be an integral part of Judaism. These defenders of Jewish tradition point out that:

> We did not go into *Galut* [exile] because we did not possess a *Hagganah* [pre-1948 Zionist militia] and because we had no political leaders of the Herzl and Ben-Gurion type to guide us along the same paths. But we are exiled just because we did possess them and did follow their lead. And certainly, Jewish Salvation will not come through such agencies.[25]

Across Israel and worldwide, Jews grapple with contradictions between the Judaism they profess to believe in and the Zionist ideology that has in fact taken hold of them. A growing number of Jews are embracing National Judaism, or *dati-leumi* in Hebrew, a relatively recent form of Judaism rooted in Israel. For many Jews, this framework helps reconcile moral qualms and gives religious justification to their Zionist commitment. Although only a fifth of the country's Jewish population are followers of National Judaism, many Israelis who do not necessarily adhere to their lifestyle (whether they are secular, ultraorthodox, or traditionalist) are coalescing around their political ideology. Bezalel Smotrich, a prominent follower of National Judaism, said in 2019: "We form the nuclear reactor that provides power to all the people of Israel."[26] While he was certainly prescient, this energy has little to do with the Judaism that has been developed over the last two millennia. Followers of National Judaism may have more in common with those who idealistically embraced National Socialism in Germany and ended up committing genocide.

After the Second World War, Zionist emissaries convinced, blackmailed and even violently coerced desperate survivors, crowded in displaced persons camps in Europe, to leave for the newly created State of Israel.[27] The Zionist interpretation of the Nazi genocide has produced a powerful moral narrative. While rabbinic tradition often portrays the Jew as physically weak but spiritually strong in his faith in God, secular Zionism replaces faith in God with faith in oneself and in one's weapons. National Judaism, which later emerged as a militant religious movement, continues to mobilise divine purpose in the pursuit of the Zionist settlement. The late 20th century rabbinical scholar Moshe Sober (1955-2006), for many years affiliated with National Judaism, later criticized this human propensity to manipulate divine will. He wrote:

> The notion that we can do whatever we please, succumb to any kind of temptation, or engage in any form of foolish self-aggrandizement without fear of penalty because we have an inside track to the Almighty is the plain opposite of religious faith. [...] Such blind faith is not really a faith in God at all, but rather faith in ourselves. It makes a tool out of the Almighty. It turns him into a kind of "secret weapon" whose purpose is to guarantee our success at whatever we fancy. It is an idolatrous concept that masks what is actually an irrational belief in our own invincibility.[28]

Adherents of National Judaism have become the most active component of Israeli society, making their viewpoint bear on issues of security, foreign policy and the treatment of Palestinians. This ideological current includes the assassin of Prime Minister Yitzhak Rabin, who was killed in 1994 for pursuing a peace agreement with the Palestinians, as well as prominent members of the Israeli government, some of whom have been convicted for terrorism in Israel.[29]

National Judaism is also the dominant ideology of most of the settlers in the West Bank, including their vigilantes who have stepped up the harassment, dispossession and murder of Palestinians in the West Bank as the genocide in Gaza continues.[30] These gun-toting militants work hand in hand with the Israeli army which uses tanks, bombs and rockets. Adherents of National Judaism overtly encourage the starvation of Palestinians in Gaza.[31] At the same time, many Jews, both in Israel and around the world, are protesting against the brutal cruelty of Israel, as well as its misuse of Judaism for its own political ends. These voices call for a return to ethical principles rooted in justice, compassion and the sanctity of human life.

NOTES

1. Avineri, *op. cit.*, p. 200.

2. Yakov M. Rabkin, "Religious Roots of a Political Ideology: Judaism and Christianity at the Cradle of Zionism." *Mediterranean Review*, 2012, 5(1), pp. 75-100.

3. See: Yakov M. Rabkin, *A Threat from Within: A Century of Jewish Opposition to Zionism*. London: Zed, 2006.

4. Adam Shatz, *Prophets Outcast: A Century of Dissident Jewish Writing about Zionism and Israel*. New York: Nation Press, 2004, p. 45.

5. J.B. Schechtman, *Fighter and Prophet*. New York: Thomas Yoseloff, 1961, p. 261.

6. "Einstein on Zionism: He is for a Jewish Homeland, But Not a Separate State - January 21, 1946." Shapell Manuscript Foundation archive.is/k34Th

7. Quoted in: Uri Dromi, "Turks and Germans in Sinai," *Haaretz*, September 27, 2002

8. Kenneth B. Moss, Nathans, Benjamin, and Tsurumi, Taro (eds.). *From Europe's East to the Middle East: Israel's Russian and Polish Lineages*. Philadelphia: University of Pennsylvania Press, 2021, p. 5.

9. Yakov M. Rabkin, "From Left to Right: Israel's Repositioning in the World," *IDE ME Review* (Tokyo) 2, 2014-2015, pp. 2-23; archive.is/yKdw9

10. Jacob Boas, "A Nazi travels to Palestine," *History Today*, vol. 30, no. 1, 1980, pp. 33-39.

11. *Ibid.*

12. Jonah Mandel, "When a Nazi toured the Holy Land to find a solution for the 'Jewish problem'" *The Times of Israel*, May 2, 2019. archive.is/lyH33

13. Boas, *op. cit.*

14. Tom Segev, *One Palestine, Complete*. New York: Metropolitan Books, 2000, p. 43.

15. Judah Leon Magnes quoted in: Elmer Berger, *Judaism or Jewish Nationalism: The Alternative to Judaism*. New York: Bookman Associates, 1957, p. 32.

16. Albert Einstein, Hannah Arendt, Sidney Hook, et. al., "New Palestine Party," *The New York Times*, December 4, 1948. archive.is/9phgN

17. Judah L. Magnes, "Palestine Peace Seen in Arab-Jewish Agreements...," *The New York Times*, July 18, 1937. archive.is/FSv4k

18. "Statement to UN Special Committee on Palestine," *Jewish Guardian*, no. 3, November 1974, p. 4.

19. Judah Leon Magnes quoted in Jack Ross, *Rabbi Outcast: Elmer Berger and American Jewish Anti-Zionism*. Washington: Potomac Books, 2011, p. 81.

20. Élie Barnavi, "Sionismes," in: Élie Barnavi and Saul Friedländer, *Les Juifs et le XXe siècle*. Paris: Calmann-Lévy, 2000, p. 225.

21. Yakov M. Rabkin, "A Global Challenge to Democratic Freedoms." *Russia in Global Affairs*, April 23, 2025. archive.is/ec2FY

22. *Ibid*.

23. Avineri, *op. cit.*, p. 164.

24. Judah Halevi, *The Kuzari. An Argument for the Faith of Israel*. New York: Shocken Books, 1964, 1, 78.

25. Israel Domb, *The Transformation: The Case of the Neturei Karta*. Brooklyn: Hachomo, 1989, p. 20.

26. Yair Ettinger, "The internal struggle within Israel's new ruling elite." *The Jewish Chronicle*, October 17, 2023. archive.is/sr3a5

27. Yosef Grodzinsky, *In the Shadow of the Holocaust: The Struggle between Jews and Zionists in the Aftermath of World War II*. Monroe: Common Courage Press, 2004.

28. Moshe Sober, *Beyond the Jewish State*. Toronto: Summerhill Press, 1990, pp. 30-31.

29. Emma Graham-Harrison, "Who are Bezalel Smotrich and Itamar Ben-Gvir, the Israeli ministers facing sanctions?" *The Guardian*, June 10, 2025. archive.is/95iEg

30. Aviezer Ravitzky, *Messianism, Zionism, and Jewish Religious Radicalism*. Chicago: The University of Chicago Press, 1996.

31. Yan Gold, "Will the government send aid to Gaza? A huge mistake." Kanal 7, May 5, 2025 (in Russian). archive.is/Srh28 ;
Yan Gold, "Attack food warehouses, Gazans will starve," Kanal 7, May 5, 2025 (in Russian); archive.is/r2gel

A New Hebrew Man

THE HOMILETIC work *Avot de Rabbi Nathan* (8-10th centuries) teaches: "Who is the greatest of all heroes? He who turns an enemy into a friend." (23:1) This ideal, rooted in the Jewish tradition that elevates peace as a supreme value, is vehemently rejected as "exilic" by early Zionist settlers. These pioneers saw in such values "the fate of the weak," reflecting only the vulnerability of diaspora life. In their enthusiasm to create the "New Hebrew," they often depicted the diasporic Jew as a degraded, degenerate being. In fact, some even internalized the antisemites' hateful and stereotypical image of the Jew, engaging in a sort of Jewish self-hatred. This is how Vladimir Jabotinsky, a key figure in Revisionist Zionism, viewed turning a "Yid," a pejorative word he borrowed from the antisemites, into the New Hebrew:

> Our starting point is to take the typical Yid of today and to imagine his diametrical opposite ... because the Yid is ugly, sickly, and lacks decorum, we shall endow the ideal image of the Hebrew with masculine beauty. The Yid is trodden upon and easily frightened and, therefore, the Hebrew ought to be proud and independent. The Yid is despised by all and, therefore, the Hebrew ought to charm all. The Yid has accepted submission and, therefore, the Hebrew ought to learn how to command.[1]

Today, Israelis often describe their state as a continuation of biblical history. Many Israelis are driven by what some describe as a "dizzying claim to build a bridge the length of the exile," linking King David to the modern Israeli military.[2] Generations of Israelis have been raised with values of martial courage and pride to serve in the army, seen as essential to securing the Zionist state's legitimacy and survival. As some have noted: while most countries have an army, in Israel, it is as though the army has a country.

The leaders of the Zionist settlement in Palestine came almost exclusively from the Russian Empire. It was in Russia that the concept of the "secular Jew," a notion essential to the success of the nationalist project, first emerged and crystallised. This new concept rejected the religious dimension of Jewish identity, both ritual and moral, and retained only its biological and even racial dimensions. This is how, for them, being a Jew came to signify someone belonging to a nationality rather than a religious identity with its important code of ethics. With the creation of the State of Israel in 1948, this identity became overtly political. For decades, secular Ashkenazi Israelis held demographic and political dominance, though their influence is now in decline. Nevertheless, the militant nationalism they developed and institutionalized has been embraced by other segments of the Israeli population, including nearly two million former Soviet citizens, most of whom support nationalist right-wing parties.

What makes Zionism unique is its determination to forge a nation out of disparate, globally dispersed groups speaking dozens of different languages. Their only common denominator was their religious practise or at least memories thereof. Unlike other nationalist movements, Zionism had to create and implant a European-style sense of nationhood among Jews who were largely unfamiliar with such a concept, and to invent a new common language to unify them.

The first waves of settlers to Palestine were Eastern Europeans, but the Nazi genocide destroyed much of the population that the Zionist movement regarded as its primary "human material":

> A hatred of the diaspora and a rejection of Jewish life were a kind of methodological necessity for Zionism... not only was Jewish history in exile deemed to be unimportant, but the value of living Jews, Jews of flesh and blood, depended entirely on their use as raw material for national revival.[3]

After the Holocaust, despite the Zionist efforts to channel them to Palestine, many survivors chose to rebuild their lives in North America and Australia. Thus, with the establishment of the State of Israel in 1948, the Zionist movement increasingly turned to Jewish communities in Asia and Africa to sustain immigration and settlement. Yet the Zionist project in West Asia, which was largely modeled on European settler-colonies in Africa, Australia and the Americas, declared independence at a time when colonialism was rapidly losing legitimacy even in Western countries.

However, like the Puritans in America, Zionists were imbued with a sense of moral and historical entitlement, believing they were coming "home" to their promised land, and that the indigenous Arab population, often descried in colonial terms such as "savages" or "primitives," were foreigners and intruders to be ignored, displaced or killed. This ideological framework was reinforced through the Zionist education system, from kindergarten to the army, which has instilled in generations of Israelis disdain for the Arabs, viewed as hopelessly backward and inherently threatening. Nurit Peled-Elhanan, professor of education at the Hebrew University, concluded her study of Israeli school materials:

> Like all colonizers, Israel portrays the colonized as primitive, evil or superfluous. Israel portrays them as a racialized group that cannot change and never will change. [...] They also are portrayed as a problem and a demographic threat, as a security threat. And because they are deemed a demographic threat, this legitimates the massacres and their elimination.[4]

This narrative is not confined to Israeli schools. Zionist educational institutions in other countries have also promoted similar messages, albeit sanitized for their local environments, encouraging young Jews from countries such as France, Canada or South Africa to volunteer in the Israeli military and eventually settle in Israel.

Yet, at the turn of the 20th century, most Jews did not consider themselves as belonging to a distinct nation or race in the European sense. On the contrary, they saw themselves as an integral part of their respective nations. Those Europeans who questioned their belonging were antisemites.[5]

The link between Zionism and antisemitism is historically complex and not accidental. While antisemites yearned to get rid of Jews from European societies, Zionists encouraged them to emigrate from their homelands and settle in Palestine. Both, in different ways, envisioned Jewish departure from Europe. It is worth remembering that the same Arthur Balfour, who in 1917 expressed imperial support for Zionism through the Balfour Declaration, had only a few years earlier promoted the Aliens Act to prevent Eastern European Jews from immigrating to Britain. No wonder that the only Jew in the British cabinet at the time, Edwin Montagu, vehemently denounced the Balfour Declaration and accused His Majesty's government of antisemitism. In August 1917 he wrote:

> I wish to place on record my view that the policy of His Majesty's Government is anti-Semitic and in result will prove a rallying ground for Anti-Semites in every country in the world.

He continued:

> Zionism has always seemed to me to be a mischievous political creed, untenable by any patriotic citizen of the United Kingdom. ... When the Jews are told that Palestine is their national home, ... you will find a population in Palestine driving out its present inhabitants, taking all the best in the country, ...

Drawing on a traditional Jewish interpretation, Montagu added with pointed sarcasm:

> I certainly do not dissent from the view, commonly held, as I have always understood, by the Jews before Zionism was invented, that to bring the Jews back to form a nation in the country from which they were dispersed would require Divine leadership. I have never heard it suggested, even by their most fervent admirers, that either Mr. Balfour or Lord Rothschild would prove to be the Messiah.[6]

A profound chasm opened up between the values inherent in the Jewish tradition and the militant European-style nationalism of the Zionists. Throughout the 1920s and 1930s, the rabbinical authorities in Palestine tried to bypass the growing Zionist establishment, seeking independent dialogue and separate agreements with Arab leaders, reflecting a markedly different approach to life in Palestine.

Yet Zionists branded these Jews as traitors. In 1924, members of a Zionist militia assassinated Jacob de Haan (1881-1924), a Jewish lawyer who was promoting cooperation between the ultraorthodox Jews, mainly anti-Zionist at the time, and Arab notables. His aim was to convince the British authorities that the Zionists were no more than a militant minority who represented only themselves, and to persuade London to repeal the Balfour Declaration, which supported the establishment of a "Jewish national home" in Palestine. De Haan was shot dead as he was leaving the synagogue after evening prayers. Many Zionist settlers from the Russian Empire were experienced with political terror, a common method of struggle against the Tsarist regime at the turn of the 20th century.[7]

De Haan's assassination marked the beginning of modern political terrorism in Palestine. It also embodied the rise of the new Hebrew man, muscular, carefree, and unburdened by tradition. From the outset, Zionists scorned traditional Jews as "weak and powerless," seeking instead to forge a new archetype: the fearless Hebrew warrior-farmer.[8] They succeeded beyond their wildest dreams. While the muscular farmer may have evolved into an IT professional, Israel continues to be a mobilised society and a formidable high-tech war machine, efficiently killing Palestinians. The name of the Israeli operation triggered in October 2023, "Iron Swords," reflects the age-old Zionist ethos to live by the sword rather than coexist with the Palestinians as equals. *Ein berera*, "we have no choice," the usual Israeli excuse for violence, rings even more hollow today than before.

Israeli education inculcates the belief that had the State of Israel existed prior to the Second World War, the Nazi genocide of the Jews would have been prevented. The dominant lesson Israelis are taught to draw from the Holocaust is simple: "The Jews were weak; we must be strong."[9] This message shapes a national ethos centred on vigilance, military strength and self-reliance.

What holds together the fragile unity of the Jewish majority in Israel is a pervasive sense of existential fear: a besieged mentality rooted in carefully cultivated historical trauma, a sense of righteous victimhood, and a perceived desperate need to prevent a repeat of the Nazi genocide. The memory of this European tragedy is a powerful tool of ideological mobilisation. It is not just commemorated; the trauma is kept actively alive and regularly invoked as a weapon to support Israel's interests.

This dynamic was evident following the October 7th Hamas attack on Israel, which many in Israel described as a pogrom and the largest massacre of Jews since the Holocaust—overlooking the radically different situation of the Jews of Europe in World War II. Yet such comparisons reflect how trauma can be mobilized to frame contemporary threats and justify national responses.

This kind of fear-driven narrative is not unique to Israel. It echoes patterns seen in other settler colonial contexts, where fear is used to sustain dominance and cohesion. As American Jewish journalist Peter Beinart observes about the country of his birth: "White South Africans were just as afraid of being thrown into the sea as Israeli Jews are now."[10] Indeed, in apartheid South Africa, white settlers lived with a persistent fear of being overwhelmed or expelled by the Black majority, a fear that was used to justify repressive policies and militarised control. In the United States, settler narratives often portrayed Native American resistance as a threat to civilization itself, fueling policies of displacement and extermination.

References to the Nazi genocide as a means to promote Israeli patriotism never cease. After an air show in Poland in 2003, three Israeli F-15 fighter jets emblazoned with the Star of David flew over Auschwitz, as hundreds of Israeli soldiers watched them from the adjacent Birkenau death camp. The planes were piloted by descendants of the camp inmates. One of the Israeli pilots later remarked:

> This is triumph for us. Sixty years ago, we had nothing. No country, no army, nothing. We now come here with our own planes to honour those who can no longer be with us.[11]

The weaponization of the collective trauma continues unabated, granting Israel "infinite license."[12]

It is therefore predictable that most Israelis portray Hamas, and by extension all Palestinians, as Nazis. Public schools promote the model of the soldier as a heroic defender against "the Arabs," as the Palestinians are usually called in Israel. This term emphasises that the indigenous population belongs to a broader Arab world with over twenty states, rather than to the disputed land of Palestine. "Why don't they settle in those states instead of bothering us here?" is a common refrain in Israel.

For most Israelis, military service is not only a civic duty but also an aspiration and a rite of passage into adulthood. As Israeli scholars Charles S. Liebman and Eliezer Don-Yehiya explain:

Whereas Judaism places man's obligations to God at the center of its value system, inferring his obligations to the community from his relationship to God, the new civil religion places the individual's obligations to the nation at its center.[13]

It has been pointed out that this civil religion offers no answers to questions of ultimate meaning, while demanding its adherents to be ready for the ultimate sacrifice. Even as the ongoing assault on Gaza has prompted more and more Israelis to avoid reserve duty in protest of Israel's actions, the foundational tenets of this civil religion appear largely intact.

NOTES

1. Quoted in Amnon Rubenstein, *From Herzl to Rabin, The Changing Image of Zionism*. New York: Holmes & Meier, 2000; archive.is/b6tiN

2. "Sionismes," op. cit., p. 219.

3. Zeev Sternhell, *The Founding Myths of Israel: Nationalism, Socialism, and the Making of the Jewish State*. Princeton: Princeton University Press, 1998; archive.is/VyVxm

4. George Yancy, "How Does Israel Justify Mass Killings? It Starts in the Schools." *Truthout*, September 15, 2024; archive.is/2ecI1

5. Léon Poliakov, *Histoire de l'antisémitisme. L'âge de la science*. Paris: Calman-Lévy, 1981.

6. Edwin Samuel Montagu, memorandum "On the 'Anti-Semitism of the Present (British) Government.'" August 23, 1917; archive.is/0XTMN

7. Yakov. M Rabkin & Yaacov Yadgar, "On Political Tradition and Ideology: Russian Dimension of Zionist Ethos and Israeli Politics" *Nationality Papers,* November 2023, pp. 1-18.

8. Todd Samuel Presner, *Muscular Judaism: The Jewish Body and the Politics of Regeneration*. New York: Routledge, 2007, p. 2.

9. Presner, *op. cit.*, ch. 6.

10. Peter Beinart, *Being Jewish After the Destruction of Gaza*. New York: Alfred A. Knopf, 2025, p. 109.

11. Katarzyna Mala, "Israeli Warplanes over Auschwitz," *Reuters*, September 4, 2003.

12. Omer Bartov, "Infinite License." *The New York Review of Books*, April 24, 2025; archive.is/2ZD4j

13. Charles S. Liebman and Eliezer Don-Yehiya, *Civil Religion in Israel*. Berkeley: University of California Press, 1983, p. 229.

European Legacy and Endurance

THE FATE of the Jews has been more tragic in Europe than anywhere else in the world. Jews first appeared in Europe in Roman times. Their presence often predates that of the majority population, although this seniority has done little to shield Jews and other minorities from persecution. For centuries, anti-Jewish sentiment was fueled by Church teachings, which sought to replace Jews with Christians as the chosen people, accusing the Jews of deicide and casting them as eternal pariahs. Throughout medieval Europe, mass displacement, the killing of entire Jewish communities, and the expulsion of Jews from several countries were tragically common. Violent riots targeting Jews occurred regularly, especially during the Crusades, with large-scale massacres of Jewish communities. From the 17th century to the early 20th century, waves of pogroms became a recurring feature of Jewish life in Eastern Europe. These reflected a long-standing pattern of scapegoating and persecution that was deeply embedded in European religious, political and social structures.

This Judeophobia, in particular the accusation of deicide, was later transmuted, in the spirit of scientism, into racial antisemitism. Like other variants of racism, this ideology remained socially acceptable, even respectable, until the mid-20th century. After millions of European Jews were murdered by German Nazis and their willing collaborators across Europe, especially from the Ukraine and the Baltic countries, Europe effectively resolved its "Jewish problem" by exporting it to Palestine.

In Central and Eastern Europe, where Zionism drew its main forces at the turn of the 20th century, the prevailing form of organic nationalism was often intolerant, exclusionary and belligerent. In this part of Europe, national renewal was seen as requiring sacrifice, especially from those who did not belong to the titular nation, a conviction that, to this day, remains strikingly tenacious.

Faced with intense and widespread antisemitic sentiment, many Jews found the prospect of emigration attractive. Theodor Herzl (1860-1904), regarded as the founder of modern political Zionism, and his circle organised the Zionist movement partly to prevent myriads of shtetl Jews from migrating to Central and Western Europe. They feared that the arrival of these "uncouth *Ost-Juden*" might jeopardise their own tenuous acceptance within European society. There is more than a grain of truth in the observation that "a Zionist is a Jew who collects money from another Jew to send a third one to Palestine."

The oppression of Jews in Tsarist Russia was, indeed, more severe than elsewhere in 19th century Europe. Most Jews were confined to a Pale of Settlement, ethnically non-Russian lands along the western borders of the empire, where they faced legal restrictions, social exclusion and economic hardship. Their economic situation deteriorated even further as industrialization accelerated in the 1860s. Mostly small, often itinerant Jewish traders and artisans saw their livelihood threatened as railways were built to distribute mass-produced goods across the country. At the same time, many young Jews were gaining access to universities and began aspiring to emancipation, such as Jews in other parts of Europe.

This hope began to flicker as waves of pogroms swept through the Pale. Even though Jews were not directly involved in it, the assassination of Tsar Alexander II in St. Petersburg in 1881 triggered a surge of anti-Jewish violence that terrified Russian Jews. This fear of violent death intensified a generation later with the massacres in Kishinev in 1903, igniting further fear of the non-Jewish neighbour who might, without warning, come to rob, rape or murder.

The shock, anger and frustration caused by these pogroms at the turn of the 20th century led nearly two million Jews to emigrate, primarily to North America. These events also fuelled Jewish nationalism and revolutionary zeal, drawing thousands of young Jews into radical underground movements. Many joined parties such as the Socialist Revolutionaries, which preached and practised the systematic use of violence against the Tsarist regime.

Many Zionist settlers from Russia, particularly those who would later become leaders in Palestine, had roots in these underground socialist circles. While most socialists rejected Zionism as a form of bourgeois nationalism, quite a few, as will be mentioned later, sought to reconcile the two ideologies. As Jewish radicalism intensified, the atmosphere of nihilism and contempt for human life gave rise to political terrorism, an ethos that some of the early Zionist settlers brought with them to Palestine.

Shlomo Avineri, in his intellectual history of Zionism, points out that this movement marks "a clear break with the quietism of the religious belief in messianic redemption that is to occur only through divine intercession in the mundane cycles of world history."[1] Within the span of a century, the traditional Jewish abhorrence of violence was transformed by a handful of Jewish nationalists into a defiant militarism. Vladimir Jabotinsky wrote in the aftermath of the pogroms:

> Young men, learn to shoot!... Of all the necessities of national rebirth, shooting is the most important... We are forced to learn to shoot, and it is futile to argue against the compulsion of a historical reality.[2]

The poet Yosef Haim Brenner (1881-1921), raised in a devout Jewish family in Russia, vehemently railed against Jewish tradition. He transformed the most famous verse of the Jewish prayer book: "Hear, O Israel, God is our Lord, God is one!"—one of the first verses taught to children and the last to be uttered by a Jew before death—into: "Listen, O Israel! Not an eye for an eye. Two eyes for an eye, all their teeth for any humiliation."[3] Brenner met a violent death in a confrontation with Palestinians in Jaffa, but the spirit of disproportionate revenge he championed lives on in the conduct of Israeli soldiers, most recently in Gaza.

No other Jewish community embraced the use of force the way it did in the Russian Empire. Many Russian Jews supported radical political parties which were flourishing in the Russian Empire at the turn of the 20th century. Russian officials at the time saw Jews as the "most dangerous component of the revolutionary movement."[4]

Moreover, the reverberations of the 1905 revolution continue to affect the political reality in Israel, whose foundation and structure still reflect the concepts and realities of a bygone Eastern Europe. From the outset, Zionist pioneers projected onto Palestine the familiar clichés of old Russia: the murderous shadow of the pogroms morphed into "the Arab threat." While Zionist settlers acted like colonisers everywhere—acquired arms and assumed responsibility for defending the territory they sought to control—many perceived the Arab resistance as a remake of pogroms.

Although emigration from Russia virtually ceased after the triumph of the October Revolution in 1917, Jews arrived from Poland and other Eastern European countries where antisemitism was endemic. This migration was largely the result of the restrictive immigration policies introduced in the United States in 1924. Another wave of immigration to Palestine was triggered by the appointment of Adolf Hitler as Reich chancellor in 1933, as German Jews tried to flee Nazi Germany.

A prominent Orthodox educator Rabbi Elhanan Wasserman (1874-1941) saw an instance of divine justice in the emergence of National Socialism and the horrors it would inflict upon the Jews of Europe. In his view, Nazism was triggered by a fusion of two ideological "idolatries" worshipped by East-European Zionists, nationalism and socialism:

> A miracle has happened: in Heaven these two idolatries have been merged into one—National Socialism. There has been formed from them a fearful rod of wrath which hits at the Jews in all corners of the globe. The abominations to which we have bowed down strike back at us.[5]

For Wasserman, the Nazi persecutions, of which he would soon become a victim, were not merely historical tragedies but divine punishment, a direct consequence of Zionism.

Because the sin of embracing Zionism's transgression is seen as a collective one, Wasserman believed the punishment would be collective as well, echoing the Torah sages' conception of communal responsibility for the Jewish people as a whole. One story illustrates this worldview:

> On the road to Auschwitz, a Jew asked Rabbi Shelomo Zalman Ehrenreich, known as the Shimlauer Rov (1864-1944), why the Blessed One had caused this catastrophe to befall the Jews of Europe. He answered: "We are being punished because we did not sufficiently combat the Zionists." For, any offence against the Torah, even by an individual, will fall upon the community as a whole.[6]

In this traditional theological framework, any offense against the Torah, even by an individual, can bring consequences upon the entire community.

NOTES

1. Shlomo Avineri, "Zionism and the Jewish Religious Tradition," in: Shmuel Almog et al., *op. cit.*, p. 3.

2. Vladimir Jabotinsky quoted in: Joseph B. Schechtman, *op. cit.*, p. 445.

3. Yosef Hayim Brenner, *Hu Amar La*. London: J. Narditsky, 1919, p. 7.

4. Eric Haberer, *Jews and Revolution in Nineteenth-century Russia*. Cambridge: Cambridge University Press, 1995, ch. 12.

5. Wasserman, Elhanan Bunim, *The Epoch of the Messiah*. Brooklyn: Ohr Elchonon, 1976, p. 23.

6. Ruth Blau, *Les gardiens de la cité: histoire d'une guerre sainte*. Paris: Flammarion, 1978, p. 259.

Before October 7

ISRAEL IS the world's most recent colonial settlement. Rhodesia and Algeria are now but distant memories; South Africa is no longer under official apartheid. Whereas white settlers in the Americas and Oceania carried out violent conquests in the 16th century and Africa was carved up by European powers in the late 19th century, Zionism initiated its large-scale ethnic cleansing relatively late, beginning in 1947, at a time when colonialism was losing legitimacy even in the colonial powers of Europe.

Some, like the Israeli historian Benny Morris who has extensively documented this period, regret that the Zionists did not "finish the job" like the white settlers in the United States, Argentina or Australia, who either killed or confined most of the indigenous populations to reservations.[1]

Today, Israel controls roughly equal numbers of Jews and Palestinians—both Muslim and Christian—but their rights are far from equal. Palestinians living under Israeli control in the occupied territories lack basic political rights. Reputable human rights organisations, both within Israel and internationally, have concluded that Israel is practising a form of apartheid.[2]

Within Israel's recognized borders, Arab Israeli citizens—Muslim and Christian—make up about 20% of Israel's citizens, yet they own less than 3% of the land. While Arab citizens have formal citizenship, including voting rights, they face systemic discrimination and exclusion. This stark disparity is also reflected in public spending on education and healthcare. For example, infant mortality among Arab children under 12 months is twice as high as among Jewish children.[3]

On the other hand, Palestinians in the West Bank, Gaza and East Jerusalem endure entirely different legal and political regimes, without citizenship, freedom of movement or access to basic services. They are subject to arbitrary arrest under the colonial measure of "administrative detention," and thousands have been held without trial for years. Palestinians on the occupied territories also endure recurrent settlers' violence and are rarely protected by Israeli occupation forces. These layered inequalities reflect a deeply entrenched system of ethnonational separation.

For nearly a century, socialist ideology constituted the mainstream of the Zionist movement in Palestine. Some socialists struggled to reconcile their socialist ideals with the realities of settler colonialism, but most readily embraced the project of building a separate society that excluded the indigenous population. This is what led the late Zeev Sternhell (1935-2020), a renowned authority on Zionist political history, to coin the term "Nationalist Socialism"—to distinguish it from to the infamous National Socialism. Sternhell argued that the Zionist variety of socialism was a far cry from socialist ideals of universalism, but rather a tool for nation-building and territorial expansion, driven by exclusive ethnic nationalism.

It was Ben-Gurion's socialist government that rejected the U.N.'s repeated demands that the Palestinian refugees be allowed to return to their homes. That same government also devised legal mechanisms, such as the status of "present absentees," to dispossess Palestinians who remained within Israel's borders after 1948. Nationalist Socialism subjected Palestinians to 18 years of military rule before granting them citizenship. Cloaking their policies in progressive rhetoric, Israel's socialist governments—in power between 1948 and 1977—received the support of the Socialist International.[4]

In contrast, the nationalist right, which has dominated Israeli politics since 1977, with only a few interruptions, makes little effort to conceal or disguise its intentions. Before joining Netanyahu's government in December 2022, the extreme-right parties openly declared their demands and required the prime minister to sign his commitment to uphold them.[5] One such demand, the policy of limiting judicial power, led to mass demonstrations across the country. Yet these demonstrations, which lasted for months and emphasized the importance of an apolitical justice system, did not address the ongoing oppression of Palestinians.[6] In fact, protesters boasted of their own Zionist credentials and military exploits, underscoring that domination of the Palestinians has broad societal consensus in Israeli society.

The word "fascist" is no longer used merely as an insult thrown into the heat of political battle. Yitzhak Herzog, who would become the president of Israel in 2021, warned a few years before then that "fascism is touching the margins of our society." While other mainstream politicians have expressed the same concern, in stark contrast Bezalel Smotritch, finance minister since 2022 and leader of the Religious Zionist Party, has proudly declared himself a "fascist homophobe."[7] A rising star in Israeli politics is May Golan, an anti-immigration activist who was appointed minister for social equality. She belongs to the new generation of politicians who are known for their direct and unapologetic rhetoric. At a public rally in 2013, she declared: "If I am racist for wanting to defend my country and for wanting to protect my basic rights and security, then I'm a proud racist."[8] A year earlier, her colleague Miri Regev, former brigadier general and IDF spokesperson, referred to Sudanese refugees in Israel as "a cancer in the nation's body" and declared that she "is proud to be a fascist."[9] She was later appointed minister of culture. In 2014, just before assuming the role of minister of justice, Israeli parliamentarian Ayelet Shaked said about Palestinians in Gaza:

> They have to die and their houses should be demolished so that they cannot bear any more terrorists. They are all our enemies, and their blood should be on our hands. This also applies to the mothers of the dead terrorists.[10]

These Israeli politicians embody an important political trend that extends beyond national borders. They often operate outside of the conventions of liberal democracy and may be seen as emblematic, if not a harbinger, of broader shifts occurring in Western societies. Anthony Loewenstein, Australian Jewish author and journalist, observed: "Ethnonationalist ideology grows when accountable democracy withers. Israel is the ultimate model and goal."[11] European history shows that ethnic nationalism can indeed easily slide into fascism, and Israel's political trajectory increasingly reflects that process.

Meanwhile, left-wing Zionism—once dominant in Israeli politics—is in steep decline. With only a handful of representatives remaining in the Knesset, it has become a political oxymoron. In this sense, Israel may be a trendsetter: authoritarianism and ethnic nationalism are on the rise in many erstwhile liberal democracies around the world.

At the same time, vestiges of left-wing Zionism continue to serve useful purposes. When the Israeli government prepared its defence against genocide charges before the International Court of Justice in January 2024, it appointed the task to Aharon Barak, former president of Israel's Supreme Court. Barak, long associated with progressive Zionism, and for that reason reviled by members of Netanyahu's government, was nonetheless entrusted by Netanyahu himself. The decision reflects a pragmatic understanding: what passes for the left in Israel remains firmly committed to Zionism.

Israel is a state without clearly defined borders. Geographically, it has expanded through military conquest and colonisation. The Zionist movement and successive Israeli governments have gone to great lengths to avoid defining the borders they envisage for the state. Israel's intelligence services and army pay no heed to borders and routinely operate beyond its declared boundaries, striking targets in neighbouring countries and elsewhere at will. At the time of writing (summer 2025), Israeli forces occupy parts of Lebanon and Syria, in addition to the West Bank and Gaza. The Israel military regularly conducts airstrikes and covert operations in Lebanon, Syria, Yemen, and Iran. This stems from the rogue state's sense of impunity, bred and reinforced by unshakable Western support and complicity.

These actions evoke the official anthem of Betar (the Revisionist Zionist youth movement mentioned earlier). Written by Betar's founder, Vladimir Jabotinsky, in the early 1920s, the anthem declares:

> Two banks has the Jordan—this is ours, that is too. If my land has become poor and small, it is mine from its head to its end, stretching from the sea to the wilderness, and the Jordan, the Jordan in the middle.[12]

The slogan "Greater Land of Israel," usually understood as the territory between the Jordan River and the Mediterranean Sea, which has been occupied by the IDF since 1967, may seem modest in comparison.

This borderless character is also reflected in Israel's claim to be not merely a state of its citizens, but as a state of the Jewish people worldwide.[13] This framing has led to the open transformation of major Jewish organisations around the world into vocal advocates and lobby groups for Israeli state interests, such as AIPAC (American Israel Public Affairs Committee) in the US or the CRIF (*Conseil représentatif des institutions juives de France*) in France. In the US, for example, the Israel lobby secures Israel's interests in American elections at every level, from local school boards to the White House.[14] Yet this scope of foreign political interference attracts far less criticism and scrutiny in mainstream media, especially when compared to the alarm surrounding alleged Chinese or Russian meddling. Only recently, the Netherlands became the first NATO country to name Israel as a threat to its national security.[15]

Israel also feels entitled to interfere in the internal affairs of other countries by demanding the suppression of pro-Palestinian activism. In close coordination with Israel, Zionist organisations such as Canary Mission, Betar, and The Israel Project have developed sophisticated methods for monitoring and targeting pro-Palestinian students, critical academics and university curricula.[16]

These groups compile detailed profiles, often using social media and public records, which are then shared with government agencies, educational institutions and employers. These institutions, in turn, have imposed sanctions ranging from university expulsion to deportation. Betar has openly claimed to have provided hundreds of names of visa holders and naturalized citizens to the Trump administration, advocating for their deportation, based on alleged support for designated terrorist organizations.[17] The United States and Germany are currently the undisputed leaders of this repression. The consequences for pro-Palestinian activists have been severe: individuals have been fired, banned from public events, expelled from academic institutions, arrested and deported.

The predicament of Palestinians in the West Bank is dire. They face repression from multiple sources: the Israeli army, its Palestinian Authority subcontractors and armed Zionist settlers. Arbitrary detention without trial, dispossession, roadblocks, segregated roads, warrantless house searches and fatalities have become increasingly common. Pogroms by settler vigilantes are claiming hundreds of Palestinian lives, further intensifying the ethnic cleansing that has long been underway.

Even before the current genocide, the situation in Gaza, often described as "the world's largest open-air prison" was much worse. Israel, in cooperation with Egypt, controlled every entry and exit and determined the amount of food and medicine allowed in. Employment opportunities were scarce, and more than two million people lived without prospects of normal life. In 2007, the people of Gaza described themselves as "prisoners for life," enduring conditions of unimaginable misery: 80% depended on international aid, water was rationed, electricity was only available for two hours a day and food shortages were chronic.[18] Peaceful demonstrations by Gazans were met with deadly fire from Israeli soldiers stationed across the border fence. Gaza was also subjected to regular military incursions, which the Israelis referred to as "mowing the grass," operations that routinely left hundreds of dead and wounded. This metaphor embodies the dehumanisation of Palestinians and the disregard for their lives. It is hardly surprising that the resulting pressure cooker culminated with an eruption of violence as it did on October 7, 2023.

NOTES

1. Benny Morris, "On Ethnic Cleansing." *New Left Review*, March/April 2024; archive.is/k9CVV

2. "World Court Finds Israel Responsible for Apartheid." Human Rights Watch, July 19, 2024; archive.is/vprVY

3. Donald MacIntyre, "Secret paper reveals EU broadside over plight of Israel's Arabs," *Independent*, December 27, 2011; archive.is/IDIwO

4. Yakov M. Rabkin, "Zionism and Marxism," in: Kerstin Knopf, Detlev Quintern, eds., *From Marx to Global Marxism Eurocentrism, Resistance, Postcolonial Criticism*. Trier: Wissenschaftlicher Verlag, 2020, pp. 123-142.

5. Michael Bachner, "Netanyahu, Smotrich sign deal handing far-right party sweeping powers over West Bank." *The Times of Israel*, December 1, 2022; archive.is/oPHCv

6. Ohad Zwigenberg, "Protests against Israel's judicial overhaul kick off at Supreme Court a day before crucial hearing." *AP News*, September 11, 2023; archive.is/LB0A2

7. "Israel's Far-right Finance Minister Says He's 'A Fascist Homophobe' but 'Won't Stone Gays.'" *Haaretz*, January 16, 2023; archive.is/0DTLs

8. Chris McGreal, "Israel: self-proclaimed 'racist' politician nominated as New York consul general." *The Guardian*, April 20, 2023; archive.is/no08a

9. Asher Schechter, "How Likud MK Miri Regev Talked Her Way to the Top." *Haaretz*, December 21, 2012; archive.is/8LPEB

10. "'Mothers of all Palestinians should also be killed,' says Israeli politician." *Daily Sabah*, Juky 14, 2014; archive.is/ISsY1

11. Antony Loewenstein, *The Palestine Laboratory: How Israel Exports the Technology of Occupation Around the World*. London: Verso, 2023. archive.is/njIIS

12. "Shtei Gadot La'Yarden" (Two Banks to the Jordan), Jewish Songs with Translations, June 30, 2024; youtu.be/fl0dVOa5NBw

13. "Basic-Law: Israel - The Nation State of the Jewish People." Knesset website; archive.is/1jbfA

14. John J. Mearsheimer and Stephen M. Walt, "The Israel Lobby," *London Review of Books*, March 23, 2006; archive.is/XBplm

15. "Netherlands lists Israel as a threat to its national security for the first time." *TRT Global*, July 28, 2025; archive.is/lKk7x

16. Anna Betts, "Pro-Israel group says it has 'deportation list' and has sent 'thousands' of names to Trump officials." *The Guardian*, March 14, 2025; archive.is/4gJy1

17. "What is Betar US, the group pushing to deport pro-Palestinian students?" *Al Jazeera*, March 25, 2025; archive.is/kXoIj

18. Denis Sieffert, "Les désastres d'une mémoire sélective." *Politis*, no. 1794, Jan. 25-31, 2024, p. 13; archive.is/orrIJ

Revenge and Survival

ISRAELI ACTIONS against the Palestinians since October 2023 reflect the main points of the *Decisive Plan* presented by Bezalel Smotrich in 2017, then a backbench Knesset member. Born and raised on the territories occupied by Israel in 1967, Smotrich was educated in leading institutions aligned with the ideology of National Judaism or *dati leumi*, as referenced earlier. A long-time pro-settlement activist, he was briefly detained by Israeli security services in 2005 on suspicion of terrorism. Smotrich was later appointed the finance minister and the official in charge of the administration of the West Bank.

Smotrich's plan asserts that Jewish and Palestinian national aspirations do not allow for compromise, reconciliation or partition.[1] Rather than maintaining the illusion of a possible political agreement, the plan calls for decisive unilateral action: full annexation of the West Bank and a strong ultimatum to Palestinians where they must choose between an officially inferior legal status if they stay, or emigration. Any armed resistance is to be treated as terrorism, and in Smotrich's words, in response Palestinians must be "killed if necessary," including civilians and children. Moreover, he rejects as a lie the idea that terrorism derives from despair. "Terrorism derives from hope—a hope to weaken us."[2] Smotrich's approach has gained significant traction.

The Israeli public has largely embraced his framing, dismissing any mention of the Palestinian suffering as an attempt to justify terrorism. The Hamas attack of 2023 offered a pretext to implement the *Decisive Plan*, normalizing extreme measures, including mass displacement and terrorising and starving more than two million people in Gaza.[3] Concurrently, Israeli forces in cooperation with settler vigilantes have intensified anti-Palestinian violence in the West Bank with the purpose of ethnically cleansing it.[4]

The shift toward the nationalist right in Israeli society did not begin with the Hamas attack in October 2023. Israeli youth in particular appear to diverge from their Jewish counterparts worldwide. While young Jews, particularly in the United States, which has the largest population of Jews outside of Israel, tend to be more progressive than their parents, embracing values of social justice and political equality,[5] Israeli youth have increasingly adopted more combative and anti-Arab attitudes.[6] One example speaks volumes. A teacher in a Tel Aviv school circulated an article from the Israeli newspaper *Haaretz* arguing that Israelis should be informed about the massive destruction the army was unleashing on the civilian population of Gaza. Initially fired from her position, the teacher won her case in the labour court. But upon her return to school, she was booed by the pupils: "Traitor, go back home!"[7] This incident reflects a broader climate in Israel in which dissenting voices—especially those expressing empathy for Palestinians—are marginalized or vilified. *Haaretz* remains the only legacy newspaper to regularly document, criticize and reflect on the path the country has taken.

At the same time, young Jews in the United States are at the forefront of pro-Palestinian activism. Many have rallied behind Zohran Mamdani, a young Muslim socialist and New York State Assembly member who in June

2025 won the Democratic nomination to become the mayor of New York. Nearly a half of Jewish voters said they would vote for Mamdani, including 67% of Jewish voters aged 18 to 44. Mamdani's criticism of Israel is reported to have strengthened his support among New York Jewish voters.[8]

This contrasts greatly with the reality in Israel. The justification for the destruction of Gaza draws heavily on the fear of another Holocaust, inculcated in the Israeli school system. According to mainstream Israeli discourse, just as the Nazis were driven by an unprovoked and irrational hatred of Jews, so too are the Palestinians. According to this logic, the Hamas attack is attributed solely to innate antisemitism. No other explanation is acceptable, and those who point the finger at Israel's suffocation of Gaza since 2006, let alone mention the *Nakba* ("catastrophe" in Arabic denoting the massive ethnic cleansing of 1947-1949) and the apartheid system imposed from the outset, are silenced and even persecuted. When Israelis point out that the number of Jews killed by Hamas on October 7 was the highest in a single day since the Holocaust, this macabre comparison reinforces the idea that antisemitism is the sole driver of Palestinian resistance. This framing also leaves no room for political or historical context and serves to delegitimize any attempt to understand the roots of the conflict beyond moral absolutes.

This attitude sharply underscores the self-righteousness and feigned innocence typical of all colonial regimes when confronted with resistance from the native population. It stands in contrast to the Judaic dictum of "examine your own actions!"—a call to reflect and pay close attention to the root causes of calamity. The annihilation of Gaza reveals Israel's character as a colonial settlement based on exclusion and oppression. Many Jews deplore this practise because it contradicts their understanding of Judaism, namely the values of humility, compassion and benevolence. They recognise that those Jews—indeed, the vast majority of them in its earlier days—who rejected Zionism for over a century may well have been right.

The genocide in Gaza was preceded by decades of "pacification of the natives." Since 2023, the Israeli *hasbara* (public relations or propaganda) has focused on the Hamas attack. Yet Hamas, originally organised with the help of the Israeli security services in the late 1980s as a counterweight to the Palestinian Liberation Organization (PLO), is reacting to decades of misery.[9] Its root cause is the siege of over two million people in Gaza and the continuing dispossession of Palestinians throughout the occupied territories. But this root cause hardly appears in mainstream Israeli and Western media, as if it all began on October 7, 2023.

Press coverage of the Palestinians is tightly controlled through various mechanisms and remains extraordinarily effective. The spectre of accusations of antisemitism hangs over journalists, whose careers suffer if their narratives, or even their choice of terminology, deviate from Israel's official line. To prevent such deviations, CNN, for example, has required its journalists covering events in Israel and Palestine, and their global reverberations, to have their material validated by CNN's Jerusalem bureau. This system is known as "Jerusalem Second Eyes."[10] It not only ensures that CNN's reporting conforms to the dominant Israeli discourse, but also with the rules of Israeli military censorship. Some prominent Western media outlets even employ former IDF personnel.[11] This stronghold appeared to crack in late July 2025, when a number of mainstream media outlets were allowed, in line with some Western politicians, to use the word "genocide" to describe Israel's actions.

Israel presents the Hamas attack of October 7, 2023, as an existential threat. Of course, a one-off raid, however bold and brutal, poses no such threat. What Hamas certainly succeeded in doing was shaking public confidence in the state's ability to protect its citizens. This also undermines the claim that the Zionist state represents the pinnacle of Jewish history and the safest refuge for the Jews.

The Israeli population, with a few exceptions, reacted with steely resolve to terrorize, expel or exterminate all Gazans. "There are no innocents in Gaza" became a common Israeli refrain. The massive, indiscriminate bombing and deliberate starvation are not only acts of revenge but also a considered strategic action aimed at emptying the Gaza Strip of its inhabitants. In fact, starvation is always deliberate, it cannot happen by accident, and certainly not while trucks carrying humanitarian assistance are being blocked from reaching those in need. Over a thousand trucks full of food and medicine were simply burnt by Israeli military.[12]

The bombing of hospitals, bakeries and water purification plants are proof, if there is any needed, that this genocide is part of a plan. It began in 2006, when Israeli policy was summed up by Dov Weisglass, an adviser to then-Prime Minister Ehud Olmert: "The idea is to put the Palestinians on a diet, but not to make them die of hunger."[13] Once food is weaponized, genocide follows.

When Israel claims to be the "state of all the Jews,"[14] it effectively takes Jews worldwide hostage to its policies and actions. When Jewish organizations around the world unconditionally "stand with Israel," they act as proxies for Israel rather than as representatives of their respective Jewish communities. To be more precise, they represent those Jews who identify with Israel in the spirit of "my country, right or wrong," an expression of unconditional patriotism and blind loyalty.

This "Israelism"[15]—a vicarious identification with the Zionist state, cultivated in many Jewish schools, summer camps, and youth movements—has, in many cases, supplanted traditional Jewish identity, in part because this new identity is less demanding. Traditional Jewish identity is rooted in adherence to Torah commandments and encompasses both private and public behaviour and actions. Israelism, by contrast, imposes no moral or ritual obligations, while conveying a strong sense of belonging and collective pride. According to Israeli intellectual Boaz Evron (1927-2018), "this moral identification with power politics is tantamount to idolatry," especially since, in his view, "Zionism is, in truth, a negation of Judaism."[16] While official Jewish organisations in Western countries remain steadily pro-Israel, some Jewish Zionists seem to be having second thoughts about their identification with the state. This reappraisal is driven in part by the rising numbers of antisemitic acts in Western countries, but also the constant flow of painful images of Palestinian suffering that confront viewers on their screens.

The destruction of Gaza remains largely invisible to, or dismissed by, Zionists who organise community parades and events in support of Israel across many Western cities. These gatherings, often featuring Israeli flags and public displays of solidarity, aim to rally support for Israel but rarely acknowledge the suffering of Palestinians.

American theologian Marc Ellis has argued that "collective pride implies collective guilt,"¹⁷ a claim that adherents of Israelism vehemently reject as a manifestation of antisemitism.

It is, of course, unequivocally wrong and antisemitic to blame and attack Jews *as* Jews for the actions of the Israeli state. However, many Jewish organizations, synagogues and Jewish retirement homes have long displayed Israeli flags, usually alongside flags from their respective countries, from a time when these wouldn't have caused much attention. In moments of heightened violence, these symbols can become flashpoints. Attacks on such institutions, though reprehensible, are often interpreted solely as antisemitic, without acknowledging how the public conflation of Jews with Israel may provoke such acts.

In November 2023, an Orthodox Jewish school in Montreal was shot at multiple times, though there are no Israeli symbols anywhere in the vicinity; indeed, such symbols would be at odds with the school's religious values and ideological stance. Similarly, in Italy in July 2025, a Jewish father and his son—both wearing kippahs (the author of this book also wears one)—were assaulted. These incidents, and examples abound, underscore the rise in attacks on visibly Jewish individuals and institutions worldwide.

The conflation between Jews and Israel creates a fraught and ambiguous space. On the one hand, it is unequivocally unjust and dangerous to target Jews for the actions of another state. On the other, the public alignment of Jewish institutions with Israel, combined with their marginalization of pro-peace and pro-Palestinian Jewish voices, certainly contributes to perceptions of complicity.

NOTES

1. "Israel's Decisive Plan." Hashiloach Frontlines, September 7, 2014; archive.is/gUtKg

2. Orly Noy, "The Israeli public has embraced the Smotrich doctrine." *+972 Magazine*, November 10, 2023; archive.is/vd85p

3. *Ibid.*

4. Jeremy Bowen, "Bowen: Israeli settlers intensify campaign to drive out West Bank Palestinians," *BBC News*, August 10, 2025; archive.is/mVZp7

5. Laura Silver, "Younger Americans stand out in their views of the Israel-Hamas war." Pew Research Center, April 2, 2024; archive.is/RbWrb

6. "Israeli press review: Report finds widespread racism among Israel's youth." *Middle East Eye*, February 19, 2021; archive.is/Z3RgQ

7. Or Kashti, "Students' Demonstrations Against Reinstated Teacher Who Criticized Israeli Army Prevent His Return to Teaching." *Haaretz*, January 24, 2024; archive.is/KoBe3

8. Shira Li Bartov, "Mamdani holds wide edge among Jewish voters in new NYC mayoral race poll." *The Times of Israel*, July 31, 2025; archive.is/ruytM

9. Jeremy Scahill, "On the Record with Hamas." *Drop Site*, July 9, 2024; archive.is/KWqU2

10. Daniel Boguslaw, "CNN Runs Gaza Coverage Past Jerusalem Team Operating Under Shadow of IDF Censor." *The Intercept*, January 4, 2024; archive.is/1C4eN

11. Efe Ozkan, "Former Israeli spies hold prominent US media positions: Report." *Anadolu Ajansı*, October 18, 2024; archive.is/bN5ZJ

12. "Israel Destroys Over 1,000 Aid Trucks as Gaza Faces Catastrophic Famine." *The Palestine Chronicle*, July 26, 2025; archive.is/4cJQw

13. Conal Urquhart, "Gaza on brink of implosion as aid cut-off starts to bite." *The Guardian*, April 15, 2006; archive.is/3YFLJ

14. "Basic-Law: Israel - The Nation State of the Jewish People." Knesset website; archive.is/1jbfA

15. Erin Axelman and Sam Eilertsen, *Israelism* (2023) israelismfilm.com

16. Boaz Évron, quoted in: Yeshayahu Leibowitz, *Peuple. Terre. État.* Paris: Plon, 1995, p. 133.

17. Marc Ellis, *O Jerusalem: The Contested Future of the Jewish Covenant.* Minneapolis: Fortress Press, 1999, p. 52.

Impunity and Protest

AS OF AUGUST 2025, over 60,000 Palestinians in Gaza, 80% of them civilians, have been killed, mostly women and children. Many more people have been wounded, and thousands more are believed to be buried under the rubble. Two million Palestinians have been displaced, a figure that far exceeds the entire history of Palestinian expulsions since the onset of Zionist colonisation. As Israel attacks hospitals and civilian infrastructure, infectious disease and famine claim even more lives. The violent bombardment of Gaza has devastated the area, with hospitals, schools and power stations in ruins. There is also strong evidence that the Israeli military has particularly targeted journalists, rescue workers, doctors and academics.[1]

Israel has long enjoyed a high degree of impunity. Despite its rejection of dozens of UN resolutions, the deliberate sinking of the USS *Liberty* with its crew in 1967, the theft of uranium-235 from Pennsylvania and of five French military boats in the 1960s, the violation of the Limited Test Ban Treaty in 1979 and many other illegal exploits, Israel has enjoyed firm diplomatic and military support of the United States and most Western countries. Severe sanctions are imposed on Iran for its civilian nuclear enrichment programme, while Israel faces no consequences for its undeclared military nuclear arsenal.

This impunity is rooted not only in the weaponization of collective trauma, particularly the legacy of the Nazi genocide in Europe, but also in the fact that Israel is still widely viewed as a bulwark of Western influence and geopolitical interests in the Middle East. Political and economic links remain strong,[2] while anti-Muslim and anti-Arab sentiment in several countries creates a natural sense of alignment with Israel. The reasons for this complicity and, more generally, for the support for Israel by the ruling classes in many countries of the world, certainly deserve deeper investigation.

Western support for Israel is extensive and multifaceted. It includes the supply of munitions used in the war in Gaza, the presence of navy vessels to protect Israel, the interception of missiles directed at Israel and repeated US vetoes in the UN Security Council. Israel and the United States are "joined at the hip."[3] In Germany, support for Israel is elevated to the level of a *Raison d'État* that overrides all other considerations of a legal or moral kind.[4] Europe, while sometimes rhetorically critical of Israel, nonetheless criminalises pro-Palestinian activities as manifestations of antisemitism or support for terrorism and stifles free debate on Israel.

Israel's impunity also reflects the impotence of the rest of the world. While Muslim and Arab governments have denounced and protested Israel's destruction of Gaza, none has imposed economic, let alone military, sanctions. Turkey, for example, despite its president's fiery vitriol directed at Israel, has not cut vital energy supplies passing through its territory to Israel. Only a handful of countries have fully severed diplomatic ties with Israel over its war on Gaza. As of August 2025, Bolivia, Colombia, Nicaragua, and Belize have cut all diplomatic ties, while Bahrain, Brazil, Chad, Chile, Honduras, Jordan, Turkey and South Africa maintain diplomatic ties but have recalled their ambassadors. Russia, China and much of the Global South, have expressed strong disapproval of the scale of destruction and civilian suffering in Gaza, but as of this writing, these governments have taken no concrete steps to halt the violence.

However, there are signs of a shift on the international stage. France, Malta, Canada and the United Kingdom have announced plans to formally recognize Palestine as a state, some with conditions. These would be the first major Western states to do so. This move has triggered strong backlash from Israel and its closest ally, the United States. President Donald Trump has threatened Canada with economic retaliation,[5] while Israel is reportedly considering halting security cooperation with the UK.[6]

This emerging diplomatic narrative is new, and its practical impact remains to be seen. While recognition of Palestinian statehood by Western powers is a symbolic and political milestone, it does little to alleviate the immediate suffering and death of Gazans. Meanwhile, as of August 2025, the Israeli government, despite criticism from its own military, has begun discussing a phased plan to take full control of Gaza City and surrounding areas.[7] The plan has raised alarm among humanitarian organizations and international observers, but the US continues to shield Israel from accountability, alongside the complacent non-action of other countries, who offer little more than rhetorical condemnation.

Israel's stance after October 7, 2023 can be compared to that of the United States in the aftermath of the attack on New York's Twin Towers in September 2001. Just as the Hamas attack on Israel in October 2023 is widely portrayed as entirely unprovoked, so too was the attack in New York. The use of the term "unprovoked" serves a strategic purpose: it casts the enemy as inherently evil and irrational, discredits diplomacy and negotiations as forms of appeasement, and shuts down any inquiry into the possibility of other factors potentially contributing to these attacks.

This framing is not unique to Israel or the US; it is also practiced by the ruling circles in Europe. The European Union, for example, has assumed a pose of moral superiority, roundly condemning and sanctioning Russia for its invasion of Ukraine in 2022, while continuing to support Israel diplomatically and militarily. Just like Israel and the US with respect to October 7 and 9/11, Europe calls Russia's attack on Ukraine "unprovoked," ignoring its root causes.

Even leaving aside the questionable accuracy of such characterisations, Western policies reflect an obvious double standard. In the space of a few months, the Israeli military dropped more explosives, killed and wounded more civilians and caused a higher civilian-to-military casualty ratio, estimated 4 to 1 in May 2025,[8] than Russia has in over three years of war in Ukraine. The drastic economic sanctions imposed on Russia contrast deeply with the continuing supply of weapons and, at best, diplomatic appeals for restraint, in response to Israel's massacres and starvation in Gaza.

Despite the widespread opprobrium and public condemnation, the Zionist state seems immune to international pressure. Israel's contempt and disregard for international law, the United Nations and, *a fortiori*, moral arguments is well documented.

The International Court of Justice (ICJ)'s investigation into the charges of genocide is denounced and dismissed by Israel and several Western governments as yet another case of pervasive antisemitism.[9] In a dramatic gesture, in 2024 Israel's delegate to the UN shredded the organisation's charter before the General Assembly.[10] Though Israel is the only country whose legitimacy stems from a UN General Assembly resolution, it now condemns it as a "cesspool of antisemitism."[11] But the disdain for the UN is deeper:

> The same leader who on May 1948 proclaimed the state "on the basis of the decision of the United Nations" later, on March 29, 1955 claimed "it was only the daring of the Jews that established the state—and not any UN nonsense."[12]

This claim by Israel's founder Ben-Gurion has been reiterated by his successors, including Netanyahu.[13]

Israel has long been at the forefront of efforts to undermine the system of public international law.[14] These efforts have been bolstered by threats from major Western powers, including the United States and the United Kingdom, to defund or dismantle the International Criminal Court (ICC) if it did not withdraw arrest warrants against Israel's prime minister and defense minister. In an unabashed display of double standards, US Senator Lindsey Graham told ICC Prosecutor Karim Khan that the ICC was "made for Africa and thugs like Putin, not democracies like Israel."[15]

The court's president has faced considerable pressure, including US sanctions, threats to his personal safety, with warnings that Israel's Mossad was active in The Hague and posed a potential threat.[16] This subversion of the justice system is another demonstration of Israel's adherence to the old imperialist maxim "might makes right," in contradistinction to Judaism's foundational emphasis on law and justice.

The decline of colonial empires is usually characterised by increased violence aimed at destroying anti-colonial resistance. Israelis, however, do not see themselves as colonisers, and unleash violence in the belief that they are engaged in a legitimate national liberation struggle; moreover, for many followers of National Judaism the objective is a proto-messianic return to the Promised Land foretold by the biblical prophets.

Western bias towards Israel suffers from a democratic deficit: unlike the ruling class, the majority of citizens in Western countries regard the State of Israel as a danger to international peace and a threat to fundamental humanity.[17] In response to mass demonstrations against Israel and its supporters, many Western governments stepped up measures to restrict freedom of expression, dismantle encampments and stifle other forms of protest. Widespread intimidation and doxxing[18] by pro-Israel agencies are ruining careers and reputations and have led to prosecutions and deportations.

The exercise of free speech can lead to expulsion of non-US citizens if, according to Secretary of State Marco Rubio, free speech "severely undermines that significant foreign policy objective."[19] Students who organize pro-Palestinian demonstrations—many of whom are Jewish—are accused of antisemitism. Televised debates on what is alleged to constitute "genocidal antisemitism" on American university campuses distract attention from the actual genocide unfolding in Gaza. Allegations of antisemitism, interpreted as criticism of Zionism, have become a weapon of mass distraction, a tool for obstructing efforts to stop the genocide.

Support for Israel must be understood within the broader context of the disconnect between popular will and government action. This support tends to increase with income and correlates with socio-economic class. A few billionaires mobilise impressive funds to suppress criticism of Israel.[20] This reflects the growing divide between the wealthiest one percent and the rest of society, where elite influence, often exerted directly or indirectly on government decisions, often does not align with the views or interests of the majority.

This democratic deficit is also evident in electoral politics. As Zohran Mamdani's candidacy in New York gains popular support, not only the city's real estate moguls, but even anxious tycoons from faraway Silicon Valley are openly raising millions of dollars to torpedo his election.[21] Another glaring example of democratic deficit is the ongoing militarisation of the economy and the resulting dismantlement of the welfare state in Europe and North America, a policy that, like support for Israel, lacks popular legitimacy and reflects a widening gap between public will and interests of the ruling class.

The Hamas attack has galvanized the Zionist information war. Israeli officials rely on a network of powerful supporters, including high-tech executives, to ensure that the Internet amplifies pro-Israeli voices while stifling or silencing pro-Palestinian discourse.[22] This climate of censorship leads to self-censorship, as individuals and institutions fear repercussions. Coverage in Western mainstream media reflects this, where Palestinian lives clearly don't count as much as Israeli lives.

A notable example is the comprehensive study by the Centre for Media Monitoring, which in 2025 published findings on double standards in the BBC. They explained that Israeli deaths received 33 times more coverage per fatality than Palestinian deaths, despite Palestinians suffering 34 times more casualties during the same period. Moreover, the Centre documented systematic language bias favouring Israelis, suppression of genocide allegations and the stifling of Palestinian voices.[23]

The vehemence of Israel's assault on Gaza, marked by mass casualties and increasingly automated warfare, some guided by artificial intelligence,[24] is leading many Jews, especially younger generations, to denounce Israel's actions. According to a 2021 poll by the Jewish Electorate Institute (thus even pre-dating Israel's offensive in Gaza), 38% of US Jews under 40 believe that "Israel is an apartheid state," compared to 25% of Jews overall.[25] This generational shift is reflected in the spectacular Jewish-led demonstrations against Israel's mass attacks on Gaza, organized by groups such as Not in My Name, Jewish Voice for Peace (US), Independent Jewish Voices (Canada) and *Union juive française pour la paix* (French Jewish Union for Peace, France).

In July 2025, a coalition of Jewish organizations and 28 rabbis gathered outside the Israeli Consulate in Manhattan under the banner "Jews Cry Out."[26] Their protest was one of many. In 2023, shortly after the Israeli offensive began, hundreds of Jewish demonstrators blockaded New York's Central Station demanding an immediate ceasefire. A week earlier, Jews wrapped in prayer shawls staged a sit-in at the US Congress in Washington, where they called for an end to the violence and recited Jewish prayers that have sustained Jews for generations. In November 2023, at the foot of the Statue of Liberty in New York, Jewish protesters unfurled banners reading "Palestinians Should be Free" and "Never Again for Anyone." Many wore black tee shirts marked with the words "Jews Say Ceasefire Now."[27] Ultraorthodox Jews, long-standing anti-Zionists and anti-Israel demonstrators, took active part in protests in support of the Palestinians around the world. Jewish students have played an active role in pro-Palestinian encampments across US and Canadian campuses.

Paradoxically, many of these Jewish protesters, including the ultraorthodox in traditional black frock coats, have been accused of antisemitism by powerful pro-Israel organizations. It is clear that Israel does not represent or speak for all Jews worldwide, nor do the Jewish organizations outside of Israel who claim to represent a unified Jewish voice. Accusing Jews of antisemitism is becoming less and less credible as prominent Jewish intellectuals and activists worldwide, including some from Israel, continue to denounce Israel's actions and remain among the most consistent critics of Zionism.

Since its inception in the late 19th century, critics of Zionism warned that a Zionist state would become a death trap, endangering both the colonisers and the colonised alike. For these voices, especially those outside of Israel, the Zionist experiment was seen as a tragic mistake. They argued that the sooner it ended, without harm to its inhabitants, the better for humanity as a whole. The catastrophic reality of the Nazi genocide, however, altered this discourse. For some, the Holocaust reinforced the perceived necessity of a Jewish state as a refuge; for others, it did not erase the fundamental concern that such a state, born in a land with an existing indigenous population, and built on colonialist principles, would inevitably be mired in perpetual violence. Still another Jewish perspective is the traditional religious belief that only the Messiah can lead a legitimate return of Jews to the land of Israel.

Within Israel, expressions of empathy for the Palestinians in Gaza have come under scrutiny and repression, led both by police measures and social pressures. These measures first targeted Palestinian citizens of Israel, and, following the logic of any repression initially limited to a minority, then extended to Israel's Jewish citizens. An emblematic case is that of Meir Baruchin, a Jewish Israeli history teacher, who was arrested and held in solitary confinement after publishing the names of victims of Israeli bombings—his attempt to break through the routine dehumanisation of Palestinians. The day after the Hamas attack on southern Israel he called on his fellow citizens on his Facebook account "to do everything possible to stop this madness. Stop it now. Not later, Now!!!"[28]

Despite Israel's highly developed media landscape, many citizens remain uninformed or disengaged from the scale of suffering inflicted on Palestinians by the Israeli military. Public discourse and mainstream media coverage tend to focus predominantly on Israeli casualties and trauma, sidelining many more Palestinian deaths and injuries caused by the Israeli forces in Gaza. Mainstream media outlets have largely amplified government and military narratives, often downplaying or omitting coverage of the humanitarian crisis in Gaza. Investigations by outlets such as *Haaretz*, *+972 Magazine*, and *Local Call* have revealed systemic censorship and editorial pressure to avoid portraying Palestinian suffering.[29]

However, this disengagement is not universal. In August 2025, more than 100,000 Israelis, including families of hostages held by Hamas, took to the streets to protest the government's plan to expand its military operations in Gaza.[30] Former hostages and their relatives joined the demonstrations, with some calling on soldiers to refuse participation in what they described as an "illegal war."[31] As well, in July, 2025 a public opinion poll showed that an overwhelming majority of Israelis—74% of those interviewed—supported an immediate end to the war in exchange for the release of all remaining hostages held in Gaza.[32]

While Israelis remain focused on the fate of the hostages and do not typically refer to the tragedy in Gaza as a genocide, there is growing public concern over the humanitarian crisis, particularly in Israel's more liberal circles. Leading Israel human rights groups B'Tselem and Physicians for Human Rights Israel released a joint report titled "Our Genocide," accusing the Israeli government of taking "coordinated action to intentionally destroy Palestinian society in the Gaza Strip."[33] Former Israeli Attorney General Michael Ben-Yair echoed this assessment, stating publicly that "Jews, who went through a genocide 80 years ago, are committing genocide in Gaza."[34] Yet for many Israelis, the devastating plight of Palestinians remains distant or abstract, and far-right citizens and settler groups continue to support the military campaign.

NOTES

1. "UN experts deeply concerned over 'scholasticide' in Gaza." Office of the United Nations High Commissioner for Human Rights, April 18, 2024; archive.is/swfzN

2. "From Economy of Occupation to Economy of Genocide." *Report of the Special Rapporteur on the situation of human rights in the Palestinian territories occupied since 1967*, June 16, 2025; archive.is/DM0nF

3. John Mearsheimer, "The Israel lobby is as powerful as ever," *The New Statesman*, February 10, 2024; archive.is/LjxgK

4. William Noah Glucroft, "Germany's unique relationship with Israel." *Deutsche Welle*, October 15, 2024; archive.is/2tYMg

5. Chris Michael, "Trump threatens Canada on trade deal after Carney moves to recognise Palestine." *The Guardian*, July 31, 2025; archive.is/Bep2I

6. "Israel mulling halt to security ties with UK if it recognizes Palestine - report." *The Times of Israel*, August 7, 2025; archive.is/6Ab8O

7. "Israeli defence minister says criticism of Gaza City takeover plan 'will not weaken our resolve'." *BBC News*, August 8, 2025; archive.is/cal0h

8. "Israeli army admits civilians make up 80 percent of those killed in Gaza since March." *The Cradle*, May 14, 2025; archive.is/lwXjW

9. Bethan McKernan, "Israeli officials accuse international court of justice of antisemitic bias." *The Guardian*, January 26, 2024; archive.is/Gk1sw

10. "Israeli ambassador shreds UN charter with tiny shredder." *BBC News*, May 10, 2024; archive.is/Ml9l9

11. Andrew Mitrovica, "Delusions at the United Nations." *Al Jazeera*, March 30, 2024; archive.is/Wqy3O

12. Uriel Abulof, *The Mortality and Morality of Nations: Jews, Afrikaners, and French-Canadians*. Cambridge: Cambridge University Press, 2015, p.202 n 386. (NB: *Um-shmum* is a dismissive play on "UN" in Hebrew, akin to saying "United Nations, Shmoonited Nations!" in colloquial English.)

13. Simon Speakman Cordall, "Israel's 'war' against the UN." *Al Jazeera*, October 25, 2024; archive.is/XYDRI

14. Patrick Wintour, "Israel's ban on working with Gaza aid agency threatens aims of UN, ICC hears." *The Guardian*, April 28, 2025; archive.is/8k5ny

15. David Hearst, Imran Mulla and Simon Hooper, "How Karim Khan's Israel war crimes probe was derailed by threats, leaks and sex claims." *Middle East Eye*, August 1, 2025; archive.is/FISGN

16. *Ibid*.

17. Laura Silver, "Most people across 24 surveyed countries have negative views of Israel and Netanyahu." Pew Research Center, June 3, 2025; archive.is/wAAaZ

18. Doxxing is a form of online abuse and intimidation targeting an individual by making their personal information public.

19. "Mahmoud Khalil can be expelled for his beliefs alone, US government argues." *The Guardian*, April 10, 2025; archive.is/ygFG5

20. "Billionaires are teaming up for pro-Israel, anti-Hamas media drive: Report." *Al Jazeera*, November 12, 2023; archive.is/u8JIP

21. Yves Smith, "Billionaires Flail About Trying to Beat Mamdani; Wall Street Journal Describes Shambolic Plan to Spend $20 Million." *Naked Capitalism*, July 11, 2025; archive.is/FPSCU

22. "TikTok Appoints Ex-Israeli Soldier as New 'Hate Speech' Manager." *The Palestine Chronicle*, July 31, 2025; archive.is/xdSFh ; Sabyasachi Karmaker, "A case of digital apartheid: How tech giants suppress Palestinian activism." *The Business Standard*, September 8, 2022; archive.is/A4WbP

23. "BBC On Gaza-Israel: One Story, Double Standards." Centre For Media Monitoring, June 16, 2025; archive.is/7mn7f

24. Bethan McKernan and Harry Davies, "'The machine did it coldly': Israel used AI to identify 37,000 Hamas targets." *The Guardian*, April 3, 2024; archive.is/0iMrs

25. Jack Jenkins, "At Jewish Voice for Peace conference, a balance of popularity and risk under Trump." *Religion News Service*, May 9, 2025; archive.is/PeAr3

26. Email announcement, "From My Desk - Enough is Enough." Partners for Progressive Israel, (date unknown); archive.is/xILVk

27. Camille Baker, "The Statue of Liberty Is the Setting for an Israel-Hamas War Protest." *The New York Times*, November 6, 2023; archive.is/ix2bX

28. Emma Graham-Harrison and Quique Kierszenbaum, "'It is a time of witch hunts in Israel': teacher held in solitary confinement for posting concern about Gaza deaths." *The Guardian*, January 13, 2024; archive.is/fzfpb

29. Haggai Matar, "Breaking new records, Israel sees unprecedented spike in media censorship." *+972 Magazine*, May 2, 2025; archive.is/LBPbY

30. "Thousands in Tel Aviv protest against Netanyahu's plan to escalate Gaza war." *The Guardian*, August 9, 2025; archive.is/GtK47

31. Noam Lehmann, "Ex-captive's nephew, mother of reservist call on soldiers to refuse to carry out Gaza City takeover plan." *The Times of Israel*, August 9, 2025; archive.is/Eapbs

32. "Breaking with PM, 74% of Israelis back war-ending deal to free all hostages - poll." *The Times of Israel*, July 11, 2025; archive.is/JgpdC

33. "'Our Genocide': Israeli Human Rights Groups Accuse Israel of Destroying Palestinian Society in Gaza." *Democracy Now!*, July 29, 2025; archive.is/kLhna

34. Qazi Zaid, "Former Israeli attorney general says Israel committing genocide in Gaza." *Middle East Eye*, July 29, 2025; archive.is/uLRMi

David, Goliath and Samson

SINCE OCTOBER 2023, Palestinians in Gaza have continued to be killed and wounded by one of the world's most sophisticated war machines. This has only intensified the tragedy of Palestinians in both Gaza and the West Bank. Israelis, meanwhile, have found themselves trapped in a vicious circle: the chronic and inevitable insecurity inherent to settler colonialism reinforces the Zionist belief that Jews must rely on the use of force and violence to survive. This mindset provokes aggression, which in turn generates more insecurity.

It has been observed that "to stand in the way of settler colonization, all the native has to do is to stay at home."[1] Whatever settlers may claim—and they often have much to say—the primary motive for elimination is not race, religion, ethnicity, or level of civilization, but access to land. Territorial control is the defining and irreducible element of settler colonialism. The logic of colonial settlement radicalises society and can lead it down a path from displacement and ethnic cleansing to genocide.

The often-used phrase "Israeli-Palestinian conflict" is misleading, as it creates the illusion of two more or less equal parties in a struggle. But this framing obscures the profound imbalance of power. A girl resisting a rapist is not "involved in a conflict," she is defending herself against violence. Similarly, Israel's military capabilities far exceed those of all of its neighbouring states, let alone the Palestinians. The IDF is at the service of a colonial settlement that is engaged in the control, pacification, displacement and elimination of the indigenous population.

What are the possible scenarios? Most countries continue to support the so-called two-state solution as the preferred conclusion of the conflict. However, as Palestinian politician Mustafa Barghouti has argued, this support is hollow. He stated,

> Nobody can claim to support the two-state solution without the removal of the occupation; the removal of all settlers from the occupied territories; reversing the decision to annex East Jerusalem, and finally allowing Palestinian refugees to come back home. Without this, anybody who talks about a two-state solution is practicing hypocrisy. It's only a slogan to give Israel time to finish the job of annexation.[2]

In July 2025, the Israeli parliament passed a non-binding motion calling for the annexation of the occupied West Bank. The resolution passed 71-13, declaring the West Bank to be "an inseparable part of the Land of Israel."[3] This symbolic move reflects a normalization of annexation in Israeli politics. At the same time, settler violence against Palestinians in the West Bank has intensified over the past decade. One of the most notorious incidents occurred in February 2023, when hundreds of Israeli settlers rampaged through the town of Huwara, torching homes, vehicles and businesses. Major General Yehuda Fuchs, head of the IDF Central Command, described the event as a "pogrom" and accused the Jewish extremists of "spreading terror."[4]

The prospect of abandoning Zionist supremacy and apartheid structures to grant equal rights to all inhabitants between the Jordan and the Mediterranean is extremely remote. Such a transformation, entailing the full application of equal social and political rights, would require a fundamental reimagining of the Zionist state: a process of "dezionisation" of both state and society, comparable to the denazification of Germany after 1945. This would mean replacing the existing ethnocracy with a state that treats all citizens equally, regardless of ethnicity or religion.[5]

However, Israeli society is deeply conditioned to see such projects as an existential threat and a rejection of Israel's "right to exist." Nothing, not even the killing of tens of thousands of Palestinian civilians, half of them babies and children, seems to shake this carefully nurtured conviction. One hypothetical path to systemic change could involve total economic isolation, potentially leading to an implosion of Israeli society under the weight of an economic crisis and mass emigration. However, Zionist billionaires, primarily in the United States, might leverage their impressive financial and therefore political clout to buffer Israel from such isolation.

The scenario currently unfolding is part of the century-long Zionist project, namely, the total ethnic cleansing (through displacement, emigration or genocide) of indigenous Palestinians from the Zionist state.[6] A major stumbling block so far is the lack of countries willing to take in millions of displaced Palestinians. Otherwise, US President Donald Trump has proposed rebuilding Gaza as a "Riviera of the Middle East" on the "demolition site" left behind by the Israeli forces.[7]

At the time of writing, massive global protests against the Israeli genocide have had no impact—neither on the vengeful violence in Gaza, nor on the continued supply of American, Canadian and European weapons used to execute it. The mass murder continues unabated, and there is ample cause for despair. Yet Judaic tradition encourages perseverance, even in seemingly hopeless circumstances: "It is not your duty to complete the work, but neither are you at liberty to desist from it..." (*Pirkei Avot* 2:16).

Israel is perhaps the most obvious expression of the imperialist and racist elements in Western foreign policy. The wars waged by Israel are part of a broader pattern of Western colonial wars against Afghanistan, Iraq, Libya and Syria, not to mention the occasional operations in Africa and Latin America. Whether the pretext is the "white man's burden," the "civilizing mission," the "promotion of democracy" or the "responsibility to protect," it is consistently the same powers that intervene in regions inhabited by less than white "insurgents," "savage rebels," "terrorists," etc.

Many observers, drawing parallels with the precedent of South Africa, argue that strong international pressure could force Israel to change course. However, such a shift would require a significant global geostrategic realignment and the emergence of a credible threat of military action against Israel.

The anti-apartheid struggle in South Africa was deeply intertwined with Cold War dynamics. It received political support from the Soviet Union and military assistance from Cuba. This geopolitical context pressured the United States to go against its previous record and support the anti-apartheid movement, not out of moral imperative, but to prevent South Africa from aligning with Soviet interests, so as "not to lose South Africa to the Russians."

It is difficult to predict when such a balance of geopolitical forces might emerge again. Israel's military, economic and technological dominance was achieved during the "unipolar moment" following the self-destruction of the Soviet Union, a period marked by unrivaled US global influence. As long as American military supremacy remains, Israel has little to fear from the international community.

Israel has shifted from the early image of a Zionist David confronting an Arab Goliath, an image cultivated during its first wars, to that of a Goliath dominating the entire region and enjoying automatic support of the American superpower and its satellites. Yet the more fitting metaphor may be that of Samson, which the world must fear: a figure willing to take his own life to kill his enemies, a nuclear-armed Samson whose back may one day be against the wall. In the meantime, this apocalyptic scenario remains far away. Even if a more equitable global distribution of military power were to develop, Israel retains a powerful deterrent: the Samson Option, a doctrine suggesting that Israel might resort to nuclear retaliation against countries it deems to pose an existential threat.[8] Clearly, no country in the world is prepared to risk a nuclear attack to liberate the Palestinians.

NOTES

1. Deborah Bird Rose, *Hidden Histories. Black Stories from Victoria River Downs, Humbert River and Wave Hill Stations*. Canberra: Aboriginal Studies Press, 1991, p. 46.

2. Óscar Gutiérrez, "Mustafa Barghouti, former Palestinian minister: 'We can live together in one democratic state'." *El País*, May 30, 2024; archive.is/BrCs8

3. Sam Sokol, "Knesset votes 71-13 for non-binding motion calling to annex West Bank." *The Times of Israel*, July 23, 2025; archive.is/Iuylm

4. Joshua Davidovich, "Settler extremists sowing terror, Huwara riot was a 'pogrom,' top general says." *The Times of Israel*, February 28, 2023; archive.is/0KyG2

5. Yakov M. Rabkin, "A glimmer of hope: a state of all its citizens," *Tikkun: A Bimonthly Jewish Critique of Politics, Culture & Society*, July/Aug 2002, pp. 56-61.

6. Orly Noy, "The Israeli public has embraced the Smotrich doctrine." *+972 Magazine*, November 10, 2023; archive.is/vd85p

7. William Christou and Quique Kierszenbaum, "Far-right Israeli politicians and settlers discuss luxury 'Gaza riviera' plan." *The Guardian*, July 24, 2025; archive.is/spX1A

8. "Strategic Doctrine - Israel." Federation of American Scientists, May 25, 2000; archive.is/qpO2r

Strategic Conflation: Israel's Win-Win

WHILE the stranglehold of Zionist billionaires remains strong, the public's frustration at the hypocrisy of their governments in supporting the annihilation of Gaza may boil over. Anger at Israel is building among populations in many countries, but as governments balk at putting real pressure on Israel, there is a risk that local Jews, whom Israel claims to represent, will bear the brunt of popular anger. In reality, Jews, including those who identify as Zionist, have negligible to no effect on Israel's actions. Nevertheless, they have become hostages to Israel's international image. Israel and pro-Israel advocacy groups have largely succeeded in conflating Jews and Israel in the public mind.

Western politicians also frequently associate Jewish citizens with Israel. President Trump referred to Netanyahu as "your prime minister" in 2019 when addressing a Jewish audience in the United States during his first term as president.[1] In 2023, President Biden declared that "without Israel, there's not a Jew in the world who's secure."[2] Such remarks further muddle fundamental distinctions between Judaism and Zionism, between Jewish identity and Israeli nationality.

Israeli leaders actively encourage this conflation as it serves highly strategic purposes. It reinforces Zionist ideology, fuels antisemitism by making Jews abroad appear complicit in Israeli policies and may ultimately drive Jews to emigrate to Israel. It's a win-win scenario for the Zionist state: new immigrants contribute intellectual, entrepreneurial and financial resources, while also expanding the pool of potential recruits to the IDF.

Other Jews, who resent being associated with Israel and are disgusted by its actions, as well as by the pro-Israel voices emanating from mainstream Jewish communities, are distancing themselves from communal Jewish life. Many choose to practice Judaism and Jewish culture privately, within the safety of their homes. In response, new communities, some of them virtual, are emerging to bring together Jews who are deeply committed to Judaism and its values and therefore are critical of Israel and Zionism.[3] More and more, one can read "Free Palestine" at the end of messages on Jewish social media. The largest Jewish organisation critical of Israel is Jewish Voice for Peace, which has close to 800,000 members and supporters in the United States and 2.37 million social media followers. Steadily growing numbers of ultraorthodox Jews, many of whom reject Zionism on theological grounds, certainly boost Jewish anti-Zionist ranks.

Pro-Palestinian demonstrations are banned in several European capitals, where commercial or cultural boycotts of Israel have been outlawed for years. This concerted pressure from governments, courts, police, media companies, employers and university administrations is fueling a powerful sense of frustration among the public. Even in the United States, a majority of people now hold an unfavourable view of Israel.[4] According to a 2025 Pew Research Center survey, 53% of Americans express a negative opinion of Israel. This shift is especially pronounced among younger adults and Democrats, with 69%

of Democrats and 50% of Republicans under the age of 50 viewing Israel unfavorably.⁵ Yet despite public disapproval, this sentiment does not translate into government policy, as Israel continues to enjoy the backing of many extremely wealthy and, by extension, powerful people.

Israel's technologies are in high demand among the governments in both Western countries and the Global South. The unprecedented gap between the wealthy minority and the impoverished majority that can be observed across the globe makes Israel a strategically valuable partner. Its military and surveillance industries offer sophisticated tools for population control, tools that have been tested and refined over decades of use on Palestinians.

These technologies, encompassing both equipment and operational expertise, are increasingly in demand as economic and social polarisation continues to destabilise the established political order. Across regions, ruling classes require effective means to suppress citizen resistance, and Israeli know-how in this field, though undermined by the October 2023 Hamas attack, remains in high demand.

The October 2023 calamity also brought attention to a secret military order known as the Hannibal Directive. Designed to prevent Israeli soldiers from being captured by enemy forces during combat, it was interpreted as "an IDF soldier is better dead than abducted." Its aim is to prevent having to negotiate with those Israel describes as terrorists and hostage-takers. Although this doctrine was apparently rescinded in 2016, several investigations and survivor testimonies suggest that on the day of the Hamas attack, the Israeli military opened fire on Israelis to prevent them falling into Hamas hands.⁶ According to reports, Israeli commanders issued orders to prevent kidnappings "by any means necessary."[7] Former Defense Minister Yoav Gallant later admitted to authorizing the Hannibal Directive in certain areas during the attack.[8] The imperative to prevent capture therefore overrides the survival of fellow Israelis, whether civilians or soldiers. One incident involved three Israeli hostages who emerged shirtless and waving white flags, only to be shot at and killed at close range by IDF soldiers who claim to have mistaken them for threats.[9] There have even been allegations that Israeli forces attempted to kill an American Israeli hostage to derail direct US negotiations with Hamas.[10]

More than two decades ago, renowned Israeli author David Grossman addressed then-Prime Minister Ariel Sharon, whose bellicose policies were widely seen as provoking the Second Intifada. Grossman wrote:

> We start to wonder whether, for the sake of your goals, you have made a strategic decision to move the battlefield not into enemy territory, as is normally done, but into a completely different dimension of reality—into the realm of utter absurdity, into the realm of utter self-obliteration, in which we will get nothing, and neither will they. A big fat zero.[11]

This reflection captures a deeper cultural undercurrent within Zionist political and military thought, one that contains sacrificial and even suicidal elements. It harks back to the nihilist ethos of the Russian revolutionary underground, which early Zionist settlers brought with them to Palestine. Once their goal of statehood was achieved, this ethos was symbolically reinforced when the IDF chose Masada as the site for its officer swearing-in ceremonies.[12] The Masada fortress is historically significant as the location. It was there in 73 CE that Jewish zealots, surrounded by Roman legions, concluded their hopeless revolt against Rome in a collective suicide. The founders of the State of Israel strove to inculcate this heroic spirit in generations of Israelis. One may also recall that the Israeli nuclear doctrine is named after the biblical Samson, who brought down death to his enemies by killing himself. This contrasts with traditional Judaism, where rabbinical teachings value life above all and condemn suicide as alien and fundamentally opposed to Jewish law and ethics. No wonder "Ben-Gurion saw Judaism as the historical misfortune of the Jewish people and an obstacle to its transformation into a normal nation."[13]

William Hechler, the Anglican chaplain at the British embassy in Vienna who inspired Theodor Herzl to launch the Zionist movement and introduced him to several European rulers at the turn of the 20th century, confided to a Jewish friend near the end of his life in 1931: "Part of European Jewry is to be immolated for the resurrection of your biblical homeland."[14]

Ben-Gurion is reputed to have said at the Central Committee meeting of the Mapai party in 1938:

> If I knew that all Jewish children could be saved by having them relocated to England, but only half by transferring them to Palestine, I would choose the second option, because what is at stake would not only have been the fate of those children, but also the historical destiny of the Jewish people.[15]

Ben-Gurion's personality aside, the Zionist movement has long faced accusations of turning a blind eye to the fate of European Jews, except when the Nazi genocide might serve the objectives of Zionism. Some Zionist leaders actively obstructed rescue efforts that did not correspond with their political objectives.[16] The Zionist leadership has been accused of "blocking attempts to allow European Jews to immigrate to other parts of the world, in order to force them to emigrate to Palestine."[17] Indeed, some Zionist leaders did their utmost to subordinate rescue efforts to their primary objective, which was the creation of a New Hebrew nation and the establishment of a Zionist state. In doing so, they considered human beings as "human material," treating the survival, or death, of millions as a matter of political expediency.[18]

Morris Ernst (1888-1976), a prominent Jewish American civil liberties lawyer and close associate of President Franklin D. Roosevelt, embraced the president's proposal to encourage various countries to accept Jewish refugees after the end of the Second World War. Tasked with gauging international willingness to participate and aware that only a minority of Jewish survivors wanted to settle in Palestine, Ernst shared the initiative with his Zionist friends, only to face strong resistance:

> I was amazed and even felt insulted when active Jewish leaders decried, sneered, and then attacked me as if I were a traitor. At one dinner party, I was openly accused of furthering this plan of freer immigration in order to undermine political Zionism.[19]

Roosevelt's plan of resettling survivors in different countries was derailed by the Zionist movement and its allies in the United States. Since then, Israeli governments have consistently opposed freedom of choice for Jewish refugees from the Soviet Union and other countries, attempting to force them to settle in Israel.

Ernst was sceptical of the Zionist project in Palestine, "a kind of remittance society supported by the dollars of rich Americans of Jewish descent."[20] As a principled Jewish advocate for human rights, Ernst also opposed the very idea of a parochial political structure:

> I am fearful of any racial religious state. Even for those who desire such a congeries of race and state, or for those who urge it for others, it seems less than the ultimate in the development of the brotherhood of man. Nor do I believe that the thousands of years of bitter persecution of the Jewish people ineluctably proves that the Jewish heritage will not ultimately fit into the conglomerate folkways of the nations of the world.[21]

Like several other movements in post-World War I Europe, Zionism developed a moral framework centered on one sole criterion—it's utility for the collective political Cause: "Zionism was an operation to rescue the nation and not an operation to rescue Jews as individuals."[22] This prioritization of the collective Cause versus individual lives likens Zionism to a modern-day Moloch, seemingly insatiable and demanding more and more human sacrifices to this day.

While for most Israelis and their supporters, the survival of the "Jewish state," in other words, of Zionist supremacy, is an absolute imperative, some Israelis offer a different perspective. Boaz Evron, a noted Israeli intellectual, expressed the following view of Jewish continuity:

> The State of Israel, and all the states of the world, appear and disappear. The State of Israel, clearly, will disappear in one hundred, three hundred, five hundred years. But

I suppose that the Jewish people will exist as long as the Jewish religion exists, perhaps for thousands more years. The existence of this state is of no importance for that of the Jewish people.... Jews throughout the world can live quite well without it.[23]

Tellingly, Evron's secular vision dovetails with rabbinic anti-Zionism, which is categorically opposed to Zionist messianism and views the modern State of Israel as nothing more than an obstacle to redemption. From this perspective, concentrating millions of Jews in a geopolitically volatile region is seen as a perilous gamble, particularly when millions of Christian Zionists interpret Israel's role through apocalyptic lenses, viewing it as a tool to provoke Armageddon and hasten the End of Days. Evron's critique challenges the foundational assumptions of Zionism and calls for a reimagining of Israeli identity, suggesting a regional federation of Israel and her Arab neighbours; "only within such a federal structure will it be possible to overcome the self-segregating, communal and protofascist tendencies gathering strength inside Israeli society."[24]

Israel's defiant posture on the global stage is now in full display for the world to see. Nothing seems sacred or beyond bounds. The country has manipulated Holocaust memory to justify its own actions, challenged the authority of international law and the UN system, and actively suppressed freedom of speech far beyond its borders. Israel has also become a leader in high-tech surveillance, targeted assassinations and the integration of artificial intelligence (AI) into military operations.[25] These developments, according to observers and civil society groups, have contributed to a broader erosion of democratic norms within Israel and elsewhere. Many Israelis feel that they are living in an increasing authoritarian environment.[26]

Israel is also one the first Western democracies where far-right rhetoric and authoritarian tendencies have gained traction in mainstream political discourse and public life. As John Mearsheimer, a prominent scholar and world authority on international relations, has stated: "What the Zionists and now Israel have done to the Palestinians over time is one of the greatest crimes in modern history."[27]

NOTES

1. "Trump tells US Jews that Netanyahu is 'your prime minister'." *The Times of Israel*, April 7, 2019; archive.is/9O3Dc

2. Canaan Lidor, "Prominent Zionists laud Biden's remark that no Jew anywhere is safe without Israel." *The Times of Israel*, September 21, 2023; archive.is/I42LL

3. Tzedek Chicago, tzedekchicago.org ;
   Smol Emuni US, smolemunius.com

4. "53% of Americans have unfavorable view of Israel, compared to 42% in 2022." *The Times of Israel*, April 9, 2025; archive.is/y0RhP

5. Laura Silver, "How Americans view Israel and the Israel-Hamas war at the start of Trumps' second term." Pew Research Center, April 8, 2025; archive.is/UnNCn

6. Yaniv Kubovich, "IDF Ordered Hannibal Directive on October 7 to Prevent Hamas Taking Soldiers Captive." *Haaretz*, July 7, 2024; archive.is/h61fw

7. "IDF officers invoked defunct 'Hannibal Protocol' during Oct. 7 fighting - report." *The Times of Israel*, July 7, 2024; archive.is/GCoNd

8. "Ex Israel Army Chief Admits Using Hannibal Directive Against Own Soldiers." NDTV World, February 9, 2025; archive.is/ycean

9. "Israeli military says its troops shot and killed three hostages by mistake." *The Guardian*, December 15, 2023; archive.is/BmYze

10. Mohamed Khayyal, "Netanyahu tried to kill US-Israeli hostage to block Gaza truce, Hamas says." *Manassa News*, May 12, 2025; archive.is/SS8e3

11. David Grossman, "Hail Caesar." *Haaretz*, February 22, 2002; archive.is/drDoz

12. Staff Sgt. Jim Greenhill, "At Masada, a glimpse into the Israeli soul." *National Guard News*, January 11, 2008; archive.is/3Tq1B

13. Leibowitz, *op. cit.*, p. 144.

14. Claude Duvernoy, *Le prince et le prophète*. Vannes: Keren Israël, 1996, p. 193.

15. Dina Porat, "Une question d'historiographie: L'attitude de Ben-Gurion à l'égard des juifs d'Europe à l'époque du génocide," in Florence Heymann and Abitbol, Michel, eds., *L'historiographie israélienne aujourd'hui*, Paris: CNRS éditions, 1998, p. 120.

16. David Kranzler, *Thy Brother's Blood: The Orthodox Jewish Response during the Holocaust*. Brooklyn: Mesorah Publications, 1987.

17. Porat, *op. cit.*, p. 122.

18. Tom Segev, *The Seventh Million: The Israelis and the Holocaust*. New York: Hill and Wang, 1993.

19. Morris L. Ernst, *So Far, so Good*. New York: Harper and Brothers, 1948, p. 176.

20. *Ibid.*, pp. 170-171.

21. *Ibid.*, p. 172.

22. Sternhell, *op. cit.*, p. 51.

23. Boaz Évron quoted in: Leibowitz, *op. cit.*, p. 154.

24. Boas Évron, *Jewish State or Israeli nation?* Bloomington: Indiana University Press, 1995. archive.is/7TPNE ;
see also: Eliyahu Freedman, "Two scholars warn of Israel's democratic backsliding, hidden by Oct. 7's fog of war." *The Times of Israel*, July 14, 2025; archive.is/71PtW ;
see also: Haim V. Levy, "Israel at the Brink: A Systemic Crisis of Democracy." *The Times of Israel*, May 24, 2025; archive.is/55tnw

25. Yuval Abraham, "'Lavender': The AI machine directing Israel's bombing spree in Gaza." *+972 Magazine*, April 3, 2024; archive.is/fOoSk

26. "Warning About the Israeli Government's Authoritarian Expansion." New Israel Fund, May 15, 2025; archive.is/sRMl3

27. "Prof. John Mearsheimer: Can Israel Save Itself?" Judge Napolitano - Judging Freedom, July 31, 2025; archive.is/H2fvI

Postscript

CITIZENS of Western countries, who have long prided themselves on moral superiority and civilizational values, must reckon with their own responsibility for what Israel is and does. By practising apartheid and committing war crimes against civilians for a long time, Israel has become the latest expression of what Europeans and their descendants have done to indigenous populations around the world for centuries. Zionist leaders, in building the modern Israeli state, have consistently learnt from and imitated the European experience of nationalism and colonialism, including land expropriation, population displacement and the establishment of ethnically defined governance structures. In doing so, they rejected traditional Jewish values of peace, justice and compassion that have guided Jewish thought for millennia.

The genocide in Gaza, where thousands of children have been slaughtered and starved alongside their mothers, embodies the success of Israeli education in uprooting these values. IDF soldiers have not only committed these crimes, but a few have even revelled in them and made video clips of themselves doing so. This is why associating and conflating the State of Israel with Jews, Jewish history or the Jewish religion only serve to blur the picture. So does the guilt of past mistreatment of Jews or the fear of being accused of antisemitism. Whereas Jews were among the most tragic victims in 20th century Europe, Zionists have cruelly and systematically mistreated the Palestinians. Like any state, Israel must be judged objectively, on its actions and policies, something that the International Court of Justice has been called upon to do.

The genocide in Gaza brings to me personal associations. My father and his brother endured, and survived, the nearly 900-day Nazi Siege of Leningrad. When liberation finally came, my great-uncle, a doctor in the Soviet army who was part of the liberating forces, could barely recognize them. He said they were nothing but emaciated versions of themselves, all that was left was skin and bones.

Their suffering was part of a much larger tragedy, one that encompassed not only the Siege of Leningrad but also the brutal invasion of the Soviet Union by Nazi Germany and its collaborators. The blockade was enforced by land and naval forces from Germany, Finland, Italy, Spain and Norway. The Siege of Leningrad began three and a half months after the launch of Operation Barbarossa on June 22, 1941, a massive military campaign led by Nazi Germany against the Soviet Union and supported by an even larger coalition of Europeans united under the swastika. Under German leadership, soldiers from twelve nations participated in the invasion of the Soviet Union: Romania, Italy, Finland, Hungary, Slovakia, Croatia, Spain, Belgium, the Netherlands, France, Denmark and Norway. Over the course of the war, approximately two million troops from these countries joined the war effort. The German forces, including Waffen-SS and auxiliary units, incorporated hundreds of thousands of volunteers from within the Nazi-occupied part of Soviet Union, particularly from the Ukraine, Lithuania, Latvia and Estonia.

The Nazi invaders summed up their objectives clearly regarding the Siege of Leningrad, stating:

After the defeat of Soviet Russia, there can be no interest in the continued existence of this great urban centre [...] After the city is surrounded, requests for negotiations on surrender will be rejected, as we cannot and must not solve the problem of resettlement and relocation. [...] After the city has been encircled, requests for surrender negotiations will be rejected, as we cannot and must not solve the problem of resettling and feeding the population. In this war for our very existence, we can have no interest in retaining even a part of this very large urban population.[1]

The last railroad line linking Leningrad to the rest of the Soviet Union was cut off on August 30, 1941, and, a week later, the final road access was blocked. The city was surrounded, and supplies of food and fuel dwindled as a harsh winter set in. What little aid the Soviet government managed to deliver to Leningrad was strictly rationed. At one point, the daily ration was reduced to just 125 grams of bread, made with as much sawdust as flour. Those unable to obtain even this meager ration resorted to eating cats, dogs and wallpaper paste. There were even a few reports of cannibalism. Corpses littered the streets, as people died of hunger, disease, freezing temperatures or bombing.

Leningrad lost over a third of its population. It was the greatest loss of life suffered by a modern city. The former imperial capital, famous for its magnificent palaces, elegant gardens and breathtaking views, was methodically bombed and shelled. Over 10,000 buildings were destroyed or damaged. This devastation was not accidental; it was part of the Nazi plan to annihilate the city precisely because it was a major centre of science and engineering, home to writers, ballet dancers, prestigious universities and world-class art museums. In the Nazi plan, nothing was meant to survive.

On January 27, 1944 people poured into the streets of Leningrad and hugged and wept with joy, celebrating the end of the siege after Soviet forces finally penetrated the city after months of fierce fighting. Exactly one year later, on January 27, 1945, the Red Army liberated Auschwitz, a notorious Nazi death camp located in Poland.

Even today, as you stroll along Nevsky Prospect, St. Petersburg's main avenue (St. Petersburg had been renamed Leningrad during the Soviet era), you can still see a remnant of that time, a blue sign painted on a wall that reads: "Citizens! This side of the street is more dangerous during the bombardments."

The war against the Soviet Union differed significantly from the one Germany had waged in Western Europe. It was a war of annihilation (*Vernichtungskrieg*), driven by the Nazi vision of securing a "living space in the East" (*Lebensraum im Osten*), but it didn't need the people who lived there. The war against the Soviet Union was, in many respects, a colonial war.

Considered "sub-human" (*Untermenschen*) by the Nazi regime, Soviet citizens were destined to be suppressed, starved or enslaved. Their lands were to be colonized by "Aryans." To express his point of view in racial terms familiar to European audiences, Hitler often referred to the Soviet population as "Asians."

Millions of Soviet civilians—Slavs, Jews, Roma and others—were systematically killed. To name but a few examples, the Wehrmacht was responsible for the deaths of approximately three million Soviet prisoners of war; over one million civilians were killed or starved in the Siege of

Leningrad; and at least two million Jews were murdered by Nazi Germany and its collaborators in the territories of the Soviet Union.

The scale of violence during the Nazi invasion of the Soviet Union surpassed earlier genocides committed by Germany, such as the extermination of the Herero and Nama peoples in German South-West Africa (present-day Namibia) between 1904-1908. In that colonial campaign, tens of thousands were killed through forced displacement, starvation and concentration camps, methods that foreshadowed later atrocities. Of course, Germany was no exception: other European colonial powers were not to be outdone, and Britain, France and Belgium, among others, also engaged in brutal campaigns of conquest and repression.

Alas, neither sieges nor colonial wars ceased in 1945. In the years following World War II, Britain, France and the Netherlands waged brutal wars in their colonies, such as Kenya, Algeria and Indonesia, attempting to "pacify the natives," maintain imperial control and suppress independence movements through force.

Meanwhile, racism remained institutionalized and official in the United States. Ironically, both Britain and the US, though key allies of the Soviet Union in the fight against Nazism, continued to uphold racially discriminatory policies in the postwar era. Twelve years after the war, in 1957, it took the intervention of the 101st Airborne Division to enforce the desegregation of a school in Little Rock, Arkansas. To add a personal dimension to these facts: my daughter once told me about a Holocaust survivor she met in Montreal who had been liberated by Black American soldiers. Years later, while visiting Florida, he broke down in tears upon seeing segregated bathrooms.

He could not comprehend how the very men who had freed him from the Nazis were themselves subjected to repression and humiliation in their own country.

The values of inclusiveness currently advocated by the West are both recent and fragile. While explicit racism may no longer be socially acceptable, it lurks behind many anti-immigrant measures undertaken in the United States and elsewhere. Human lives are not valued equally, neither in our media nor in our foreign policies. The death of a single Israeli receives more media attention than the deaths of hundreds of Palestinians killed and starved daily.

During the Siege of Leningrad, the Nazis and their allies dropped almost 150,000 bombs and shells on Leningrad, averaging 172 per day over the 872-day siege. This bombardment destroyed approximately 16% of the city's housing stock. In comparison, and according to its own data, the IDF dropped an average of 1,000 bombs and shells a day on Gaza in the first week of the war.[2] By January 2025, 60% of Gaza's housing had been damaged or destroyed.[3] While besieged Leningrad covered a much larger area—about 14 times the size of the Gaza Strip—the populations of the two regions are comparable, approximately 3.4 million in Leningrad and 2.3 million in Gaza before the assaults. One should note that the bombs and shells are much more powerful today.

Israel's Defence Minister Yoav Gallant was clear when he declared on October 9, 2023: "I have ordered a complete siege of the Gaza Strip. There will be no electricity, no food, no fuel, everything is closed. We are fighting human animals, and we are acting accordingly."[4] In May 2024, Tali Gottlieb, a lawyer and member of the Israeli parliament from the ruling Likud party, expressed outrage towards a US decision to pause arms transfers. She warned that if Israel were not supplied with precision-guided munitions, it would resort to its own less accurate weaponry, imprecise missiles, which instead of taking down one room, will destroy ten buildings.[5] And in November 2023, Israel's Heritage Minister Amihai Eliyahu, himself a rabbi and grandson of a former Chief Rabbi of Israel, suggested in a radio interview that dropping a "nuclear bomb" on the Gaza Strip was "an option."[6] While his remarks were disavowed by the prime minister and defense minister, and Eliyahu was suspended from cabinet meetings, he remained in his ministerial post.[7]

Unlike the Leningrad blockade or the operation of Nazi death camps, when colonial or genocidal intentions were hidden or coded, Israeli intentions regarding Gaza are both public and widely publicized. Countries with heavy racist and/or colonialist pasts are active accomplices in Israel's genocide. Moreover, these same Western countries have suspended funding for the United Nations Relief and Works Agency for Palestine Refugees in the Near East (UNRWA).[8] Without delay and without seeing the evidence, this decision was taken at the request of Israel, which has long campaigned for the abolition of this agency essential to the very survival of the Palestinians.

Recalling the Siege of Leningrad against the backdrop of the tragedy in Gaza proves that the 1955 accusation levelled at the European man by the Martinique poet Aimé Césaire in his *Discourse on Colonialism* remains relevant today:

> What he does not forgive Hitler is not the crime itself, the crime against man, it is not the humiliation of man in himself, it is the crime against the white man, it is the

humiliation of the white man, and for having applied to
Europe colonialist procedures hitherto only applied to
the Arabs of Algeria, the coolies of India and the negroes
of Africa.⁹

Palestinians have long experienced this kind of colonial violence. Some thirty years ago during a sabbatical in Jerusalem, I was deeply touched by a moment on the campus of Al-Quds University in the West Bank. After my lecture, my hosts stepped away briefly to check if the canteen was open. Here I was, standing alone in the middle of a campus, when a Palestinian student approached me and said in Hebrew, "Shalom! I've never seen a Jew with a kippah on his head who wasn't also carrying a rifle." His comment moved me. I had never associated my kippah with anything violent—if anything, quite the opposite. Yet the student was clearly referring to the settlers in his midst, who now rampage across the West Bank, terrorizing Palestinians and killing hundreds of them believing they exercise Israel's right to defend itself.

American Jewish author Peter Beinart admits:

> In most of the Jewish world today, rejecting Jewish
> statehood is a greater heresy than rejecting Judaism
> itself. ... We have built an altar and thrown an entire
> [Palestinian] society on the flames.¹⁰

For this former Zionist, the destruction of Gaza marks a turning point in Jewish history, one that demands moral reckoning for the cruelty inflicted by Israeli Jews and those who encourage them to ignore all moral norms and to justify such actions "in the name of survival" or, worse still, as carrying out of a divine commandment.

Rabbi Moshe Sober warned in his 1990 book *Beyond*

the Jewish State against the movement's increasingly bellicose tendencies:

> The Palestinians will indubitably suffer more than the Israelis. That is the usual pattern in insurrections. But every dead Palestinian will only serve to strengthen their organization and every dead Israeli to weaken our establishment. It is a battle that cannot be won.[11]

Decades after Ben-Gurion and his comrades unilaterally declared the establishment of the Zionist state, William Blum (1933-2018), American author and journalist observed: "The worst thing that ever happened to the Jewish people is the Holocaust. The second worst thing that ever happened to the Jewish people is the State of Israel."[12]

I am concluding this afterword on the eve of the 9th of Av, a solemn date in the Jewish calendar that commemorates a series of catastrophes, including the destruction of First and Second Temples in Jerusalem (in 586 BCE and 70 CE, respectively), and the expulsion of Jews from Spain in the late 15th century. On this day, Jews gather in dimly lit synagogues to mourn and atone for the sins and transgressions believed to have precipitated these tragedies. Traditional Jews fast and repent, even though the perpetrators, Babylonian officers, Roman emperors and *los Reyes Católicos*, the Catholic Kings, were external forces. In Jewish tradition, however, these figures, be they Pharaoh, Amalek or Hitler, are often viewed as agents of divine punishment, an undoubtedly cruel means meant to awaken the Jewish people to repentance.[13]

Jewish teachings frequently attribute the root causes of communal suffering to internal moral failings. In this light, Israel's current trajectory—marked by impunity, hubris and cruelty, all of which contradict core Jewish values—appears destined for moral and political ruin. Whether or not that reckoning has arrived by the time you read this book, the genocide witnessed in real time has indelibly left its mark not only on the psyche, but also on the way many Jews understand themselves. Even Jews who have long rejected Zionism as fundamentally un-Jewish, and who have never had anything to do with the State of Israel, now find themselves wondering what more they could have done to stop Israel from committing war crimes in their name. This year, the 9th of Av of 2025, should remind Jews, myself included, not only of the suffering we have historically endured, but also of the suffering the State of Israel has caused in our name.

Some Jewish Israelis are slowly awakening from their moral slumber and are recognizing the humanity of Palestinians. Some have been aware of this for a long time, namely the activists and human rights advocates who have been crying out loudly for decades. An idea, likely a pipe dream, would be for Israelis to consider a collective act of repentance, especially since Gaza has become, in Trump's parlance, "a demolition site." This would mean welcoming Palestinians, treating them as fellow human beings, and help them heal from the terrible traumas inflicted by the IDF. It would mean compensating them for lost property and enabling them to rebuild lives of dignity and independence. Such an overdue act of repentance could lay the foundation for a society in which all people, from the river to the sea, enjoy equal rights.

This process of re-humanization is daunting, a process of truth and reconciliation, but it is the only scenario that can liberate both the oppressed and the oppressors from the cycle of incessant brutality. Quite a few people would qualify this proposal as suicidal. Indeed, history shows that dominant groups—whether in the American South or apartheid South Africa—often perceive equality as an existential threat. Yet numerous studies—and plain common sense—confirm that oppression fuels violence, whereas justice, equal rights and the possibility of political inclusion can mitigate it.

This year's 9th of Av, and every 9th of Av from now on, must transcend ritual fast and move beyond mere lip service to this age-old tradition. It must become a call to conscience, a catalyst to change. And so, to conclude this book, I turn to the words of the prophet Isaiah:

> You fast in strife and contention, and you strike with a wicked fist! Your fasting today is not such as to make your voice heard on high. Is such the fast I desire, a day for people to starve their bodies? Is it bowing the head like a bulrush and lying in sackcloth and ashes? Do you call that a fast, a day when God is favorable?
>
> No, this is the fast I desire: to unlock fetters of wickedness and untie the cords of the yoke to let the oppressed go free, to break off every yoke. It is to share your bread with the hungry and to take the wretched poor into your home; when you see the naked, to clothe them... (Isaiah 58:4-7)

NOTES

1. M.I. Frolov, "Leningrad wipe": plans by military-political leadership of Germany (1941, 1942)", *Nauka, Obshchestvo, Oborona*. 1(2) 2014 (in Russian) archive.is/ztYoO

2. Israeli Air Force on X, "Dozens of fighter jets...." October 12, 2023, 9:03am; archive.is/90Tgb

3. Emma Graham-Harrison, "A visual guide to the destruction of Gaza." *The Guardian*, January 18, 2025; archive.is/cSgIp

4. Emanuel Fabian, "Defense minister announces 'complete siege' of Gaza: No power, food or fuel." *The Times of Israel*, October 9, 2023; archive.is/9DPkg

5. "Israeli MK to Biden 'I'll just collapse ten buildings in Gaza'" *The New Arab*, YouTube youtu.be/oSYRWOaN5jI

6. Michael Bachner, "Far-right minister says nuking Gaza an option, PM suspends him from cabinet meetings." *The Times of Israel*, November 5, 2023; archive.is/uaP5M

7. Ariella Marsden, "Netanyahu backed down from firing minister who called to nuke Gaza." *The Jerusalem Post*, November 5, 2023; archive.is/JU8j0

8. "Which countries have cut funding to UNRWA, and why?" *Al Jazeera*, January 28, 2024; archive.is/MSXkK

9. Aimé Césaire, *Discours sur le colonialisme*. Paris: Présence africaine, 1955, p. 4.

10. Beinart, *op. cit.*, p. 102.

11. Moshe Sober, *op. cit.*, p. 91.

12. William Blum, *The Anti-Empire Report*. #82, June 10, 2010; archive.is/f1jEk

13. *Babylonian Talmud*, Treatises Megillah 14a and Sanhedrin 47a.

Further Reading

Ali Abunimah, *One country: A Bold Proposal to End the Israeli-Palestinian Impasse*. New York: Macmillan, 2006.

Shlomo Avineri, *The Making of Modern Zionism: The Intellectual Origins of the Jewish State*. New York: Basic Books, 1981.

Orit Bashkin, *Impossible Exodus: Iraqi Jews in Israel*. Stanford: Stanford University Press, 2017.

Uri Ben-Eliezer, *The Making of Israeli Militarism*. Bloomington: Indiana University Press, 1998.

Georges Bensoussan, *Un nom impérissable, Israël, le sionisme et la destruction des Juifs d'Europe (1933-2007)*. Paris: Seuil, 2008.

Avner Cohen, *Israel and the Bomb*. New York: Columbia University Press, 1999.

Jonathan Cook, *Disappearing Palestine: Israel's Experiments in Human Despair*. London: Zed, 2013.

Sylvain Cypel, *The state of Israel vs. the Jews*. New York: Other Press, 2021.

Mark Ellis, *Judaism Does Not Equal Israel: The Rebirth of the Jewish Prophetic*. New York: The New Press, 2009.

Ran Greenstein, *Zionism and its Discontents: A Century of Radical Dissent in Israel/Palestine*. London: Pluto, 2014.

Khaled Hroub, *Hamas: A Beginner's Guide*. London: Pluto, 2025.

Noga Kadman, *Erased from Space and Consciousness: Israel and the Depopulated Palestinian Villages of 1948*. Bloomington: Indiana University Press, 2015.

Ghassan Kanafani, *The 1936-39 Revolt in Palestine*. New York: Committee for Democratic Palestine, 1972.

Ghada Karmi, *One State: The Only Democratic Future for Palestine-Israel*. London: Pluto, 2023.

Rashid Khalidi, *The Hundred Years' War on Palestine: A History of Settler Colonialism and Resistance, 1917-2017*. New York: Metropolitan Books, 2021.

Baruch Kimmerling, *Politicide: Ariel Sharon's War Against the Palestinians*. New York: Verso, 2003.

Joseph Massad, *The Persistence of the Palestinian Question: Essays on Zionism and the Palestinians*. New York: Routledge, 2006.

Benny Morris, *Righteous Victims: A History of the Zionist-Arab Conflict, 1881-2001*. New York: Vintage, 2001.

Béatrice Orès et al., eds., *Antisionisme, une histoire juive*. Paris: Syllepse, 2023.

Ilan Pappé, *A Very Short History of the Israel-Palestine Conflict*. Oxford: Oneworld, 2024.

Ilan Pappé, *The Biggest Prison on Earth: A History of the Occupied Territories*. Oxford: Oneworld, 2017.

Yakov M. Rabkin, *What is Modern Israel?* London: Pluto, 2015.

Jack Ross, *Rabbi Outcast: Elmer Berger and American Jewish Anti-Zionism*. Washington: Potomac Books, 2011.

Sara Roy, *The Gaza Strip: The Political Economy of De-development*. Washington: Institute for Palestine Studies, 2016.

Edward Said, *The Question of Palestine*. New York: Vintage, 1980.

Shlomo Sand, *The Invention of the Jewish People*. New York: Verso, 2020.

Adam Shatz (ed.), *Prophets Outcast: A Century of Dissident Jewish Writing about Zionism and Israel*. New York: Nation Books, 2004.

Michal Shaul, *Holocaust Memory in Ultraorthodox Society in Israel*. Bloomington: Indiana University Press, 2020.

Avi Shlaim, *Three Worlds: Memories of an Arab Jew*. Oxford: Oneworld, 2023.

Avi Shlaim, *Israel and Palestine: Reappraisals, Revisions, Refutations*. London: Verso, 2009.

Ella Shohat, *On the Arab-Jew, Palestine, and Other Displacements*. London: Pluto, 2017.

Jamie Stern-Weiner (ed.), *Deluge: Gaza and Israel: From Crisis to Cataclysm*. New York: Or Books, 2024.

www.ingramcontent.com/pod-product-compliance
Lightning Source LLC
Chambersburg PA
CBHW020548030426
42337CB00013B/1016